S0-AXU-447

MAXIMIZING MISFORTUNE

MAXIMIZING MISFORTUNE

Turning Life's Failures Into Success

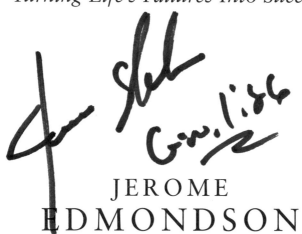

JEROME
EDMONDSON

© Copyright 2003 – Jerome Edmondson

All rights reserved. This book is protected by the copyright laws of the United States of America. This book may not be copied or reprinted for commercial gain or profit. The use of short quotations or occasional page copying for personal or group study is permitted and encouraged. Permission will be granted upon request. Unless otherwise identified, Scripture quotations are from the King James Version of the Bible. Please note that Destiny Image's publishing style capitalizes certain pronouns in Scripture that refer to the Father, Son, and Holy Spirit, and may differ from some Bible publishers' styles.

Take note that the name satan and related names are not capitalized. We choose not to acknowledge him, even to the point of violating grammatical rules.

Treasure House
An Imprint of
Destiny Image® Publishers, Inc.
P.O. Box 310
Shippensburg, PA 17257-0310

"For where your treasure is, there will your heart be also."
Matthew 6:21

ISBN 0-7684-3012-7

For Worldwide Distribution
Printed in the U.S.A.

This book and all other Destiny Image, Revival Press, MercyPlace, Fresh Bread, Destiny Image Fiction, and Treasure House books are available at Christian bookstores and distributors worldwide.

For a U.S. bookstore nearest you, call 1-800-722-6774.
For more information on foreign distributors, call 717-532-3040.
Or reach us on the Internet:

www.destinyimage.com

CONTENTS

FOREWORD

The greatest challenge in life is not learning how to succeed in life, but how to fail effectively. It is said that effective living is not measured by what happens to you, but what you do about what happens to you. In essence, your success in life is determined by what happens to you, but equally by how you respond to what happens to you.

It is my belief that all human beings face the same challenges in life, but how they respond to them creates the quality of their life. The apostle Paul in his letter to his young protégée, Timothy, summarizes this concept in these famous words; "There is no temptation that has come to you that is not common to all men…" In essence, we all have the same opportunity to fail or succeed, win or lose, progress or regress, overcome or be over-come. The key to life is not only what we do with success, but what do we do with failure.

I am convinced that a winner is simply a looser who did not quit, and a looser is simply a winner who quit. It's all a matter of response. The great wise king, Solomon of the Hebrew Old Testament, in his book of proverbs states it this way; *"The rich and poor have one thing in common, God made them both and God gave sight to both."* In other words, God created all men; some become rich and some poor, but it all depends on how they see. The key is vision. Vision is the ability to see beyond the past and present, to a future of possibilities.

No great accomplishment or great personality achieved anything noteworthy without many mistakes, failures, miscalculations, and misfortunes. Characters such as Abraham Lincoln, Thomas Edison, Thomas Jefferson, and many others who left their footprints in the sands of history, are all a study in misfortune and failure. But they overcame their failures to rise above and achieve their dreams. They understood this truth about life: **"Failure is a part of success."** They learned the lesson that misfortune and failure are only temporary incidences in life that cannot and should not prevent one from achieving his or her goals in life, but should be used as educational opportunities designed to build stronger character.

Jerome Edmondson in this exciting book, *Maximizing Misfortune*, creatively captures the power of positive perception. His personal approach through the eyes of experience provides a practical roadmap to success to which all of us can relate. His human touch in laying out the principles and precepts that can be applied to every situation one may face inspires us to believe in our dream even more and embrace the negatives as positives and turn misfortunes into milestones.

I have had the privilege of mentoring and seeing the author rise from common life to breakthrough the barriers of self-imposed human limitations, and to believe and achieve the impossible. This book is not a how-to book, but a 'follow me' program. *Maximizing Misfortune* is a personal testimony of the power of spiritual and mental revelation and its impact on a life that was relegated to the broad road leading to destruction and failure, but captured the divine truth of personal purpose and potential, and discovered that he was designed to fulfill a destiny that only he could deny.

I enjoyed reading this manuscript and encourage you to devour the timeless principles and practical advice buried in these pages. This book will become a classic that is used time and time again by those who want to achieve great things in life. *Maximizing Misfortune* is destined to join the list of required reading among the works used throughout the years for personal development. From the cotton farm to great fortune, this book shows us all how to maximize misfortune.

Dr. Myles E. Munroe

DEDICATION

"In the beginning God created heaven and earth. And the earth was without form, and void..." (Gen. 1:1-2, KJV). "Void" is how I felt growing up with no father in my life. Little did I know as a young child that the void in my life would be filled. That success in life would stem from the greatest two women on planet earth: My grandmother who raised me and my wife who saved me.

To my grandmother, Ms. Jessie Mae Redd, thank you for filling the fatherless void in my life. You taught me how to care and make do. You taught me that overcoming poverty has nothing to do with what you don't have, but how you make use of what you do have. Grandma could take a bag of flour, some pinto beans, a little sugar, together with a sack of greens she picked from the fields, and make a full-course meal that would last for days. She said, "Jerome, someday you'll have a family; I have raised two generations by myself. None of you have ever gone without a meal or clothing on your back. Take this attitude into you marriage, and you will always have." Thank you grandma for teaching me how to become a MAN who is full of sensitivity, love, and a passion to never leave my family fatherless. Through you, I broke the generational curse of fatherlessness that has plagued our family.

To my darling wife, Alena. Wow! The Word of God says that when a man finds a wife he finds a good thing and receives favor with God. When He gave me you He knew I needed a double portion of His favor. Thank you honey for challenging me to find salvation. I would have never come to know the goodness of Yeshua had you not challenged my ignorance. When the going got tough you got on your knees, and look at us now. You invested faith in me when I didn't even believe in myself. Thank you, Alena Edmondson, for standing by me and helping me to become a man, a husband and a true father to our family. You're simply the BEST!

To my daughter, Cherita, who graduated from Michigan State University on the national dean's list, and my two son's, Aaron and William, who are honor students in high school, I leave this book as an inheritance for you. You are the best children God created. Thank you for taking my tough love and discipline and converting it into leadership and obedience. Great shall be your rewards.

ENDORSEMENTS

My friend Jerome Edmondson has done us all a great favor in writing *Maximizing Misfortune*. This is a message that must be told. Everybody wants to be successful, but few are willing to pay the price for attaining success. Many will look at my life and envy the things I have and the things I have attained. From the projects in Chattanooga, Tennessee, to NFL stardom, I made many tough decisions to reach my dream. People don't realize that Sara and I paid a huge price in order to arrive at the place of success we now enjoy. It didn't come easy. A lot of sacrifices were made and there were some failures along the way.

Maximizing Misfortune is the perfect roadmap to get you on the way and help you make your dreams come true. You will be encouraged as you read Jerome's struggles in his early years and you will be sobered by the price he had to pay. In the end, you will discover some compelling and beneficial keys that will help you to fulfill your destiny.

Reggie White
Former NFL All-Pro Defensive End

Maximizing Misfortune brings back so many memories of my own struggles attempting to fulfill my dream of playing in the NBA. I watched the pain and mental struggle that my best friend Jerome endured when he was terminated from his place of employment. But it was also very exciting as I watched him turn disappointment into success. Clearly, he was determined to refocus on his dream as he sought God's direction. *Maximizing Misfortune* chronicles his success and also provides the reader powerful keys to help them realize their own dreams.

As an NBA World Champion and current NBA employee, I will use this book as a resource for the many NBA players who feel there is no hope after failure. *Maximizing Misfortune* will be a helpful guide, assisting them to be proactive in their careers to maximize life's storms.

Rick Mahorn
NBA, Detroit Piston World Champion

Maximizing Misfortune chronicles the tumultuous journey of one of today's leading Christian business leaders from the depths of abject poverty to the heights of a fast-moving, successful corporate executive, only to lose it all. But in the process he discovers God's authentic purpose for his life—calling thousands of businessmen and women to use their entrepreneurial skills to build the kingdom of God. *Maximizing Misfortune* is a 'must-read' for both veteran and aspiring Christian entrepreneurs.

Rachelle Hood-Phillips
Chief Diversity Officer,
Denny's Restaurant
President,
Inclusive Business Strategies Inc.

Jerome, your story reveals the stuff of which dreams are made. As an All-Pro Cornerback and successful member of the Philadelphia Eagles, I have had a few set backs along the way and made a lot of sacrifices.

Maximizing Misfortune tells it straight. It is not one man's theory; it is his life. I've known Jerome for more than three years. I am a board member of his organization, Christian Business Network, and I can tell you he has lived the message you are about to read. The message is clear and simple. Even though we all must face life's misfortunes, God can provide you with the power and ability to transform those challenges into success. *Maximizing Misfortune* is a must read for everyone looking to fulfill his dream. Jerome did it. I am doing it. And so can you.

Troy Vincent
Cornerback, Philadelphia Eagles

Jerome Edmondson's book Maximizing Misfortune is a prime example of turning failure and misfortune into Kingdom success and eternal significance. Anyone planning to do anything meaningful in Christ needs to read this book. It shows the price we all must pay for Godly success and greatness in His Kingdom, as well as giving us all hope and encouragement in God's overriding love and faithfulness towards us.

Bishop Eddie L. Long
Senior Pastor, New Birth Missionary Baptist Church,
Lithonia, Georgia

AUTHOR'S NOTE

This book has been written for those who find themselves weathering life's storms and feeling that they have little or no hope of recovery. That was once my life, but I found that once I made a commitment to live my life beyond the borders of my own self-interest, all my problems became challenges that could pave a path to success. If you can look at your life's storms chronologically and understand how and why they became a part of your experiences, you will come to the same conclusion that I did. You will see that success depends upon a pattern of positive and negative experiences. The way you succeed or recover from such misfortunes determines the extent of your possibilities.

Success is a choice. Once I discovered that God loves the sinner as much as the believer, I knew that anyone could become successful. Success is derived through a diligent work ethic and can be accomplished with or without a relationship with Jesus Christ, therefore there is no excuse for poverty. However, your ability to sustain and enjoy good success will entirely depend on a personal relationship with the Creator of Mankind.

Life is not your choice; you were created for a purpose higher than your own self-interest. If you don't know your true purpose, you're living on Earth illegally as a citizen of the kingdom of God. Once you discover your purpose—the business, gift, or ministry to which God has called you—you will be able to maximize every misfortune that enters your life. On the other hand, if you never find your purpose, life's storms will defeat you every time, and your life on Earth will feel meaningless and empty. You will take your potential and all the good you might have accomplished for others to your grave. What a tragedy, as Dr. Myles Munroe, my spiritual father, would say.

Your life is a sum total of the behaviors and characteristics with which you've associated your spirit along its journey. Your ability to maximize your own misfortunes will determine the level of value you will add to the mandate God has given you to perform.

Human behavior is the most unpredictable force of creation. While you can train and manage Earth's variety of animals, the human being, God's most prized creation, leaves even the most educated philosophers and spiritual leaders without answers. That's because even when every factor in your life seems to predict failure, Yeshua can take those things that are not and create a shining success. He did that with me, and He will do the same for you.

CHAPTER 1

FIELDS OF DREAMS

You might suppose that a dirt-poor, abandoned child growing up in the dusty fields of Harmondale, Missouri would have little to hold on to. But to me, those endless, sun-baked fields of cotton and soybeans produced much more than next year's crop and a promise of sore backs, bleeding fingers, and blistered hands. In those fields grew my dreams.

My grandmother raised seven of us children—five of us never even knew who our fathers were. My mother lived in New York. Within about a month of birthing each one of us, she'd arrive at my grandmother's tiny wooden shack in a big, fancy car, often with a different guy, drinking and smoking, and she would drop us off. She never spent more than six months with any of us—all seven—and then she'd go back to New York or Grand Rapids or wherever she decided to call home. And to this day I still love her.

As a little guy, it was painful for me to watch my grandmother chop firewood, shovel coal, pump water from an outdoor well during blistering winter months, and depend on welfare and generous neighbors to make ends meet for all of us. I used to go outside and try to help her, but she'd always make me go back in the house. Even when my brothers and sisters grew older, none of them really helped her. I'd run to the window and watch her chopping wood in the bitter cold. The window would fog up, and I'd rub off the fog so I could see her every minute until she came back in where it was warm. I didn't want anything to happen to Grandma. I loved and admired her so much. She was my hero.

It was at those times that I started dreaming. I would dream about helping my grandma and taking her away from all of that work and poverty. I'd dream about seeing her sitting in a nice warm kitchen with pretty curtains, comfortable and warm, with lots of good food and no cares to put deep creases in her forehead and calluses on her hands. I wanted her to have a home like the beautiful houses owned by the farmers for whom we worked.

In the country where we lived there seemed to be nothing but endless stretches of fields, dirt roads, and a great big sky. Looking into that vast, sparkling sky every night sparked my dreams. I claimed one of those stars—decided that it was my very own. It was the one right next to the Little Dipper. I would lie on my back at night, look for the Little Dipper, and locate my own star among the hundreds of thousands of glistening diamonds in the expansive black night. I would dream and dream...

I'm going to grow up and be successful—with lots and lots of money. I'll take my grandmother out of here and move her to a beautiful place where she will always be warm, where she won't have to work so hard, and where she will have plenty. She'll have the biggest, most beautiful turkeys at Christmas, and they'll taste so good. She'll pass over the chitterlings, pig feet, and pig tails at the store and select the best steaks that money can buy. She'll have electric heat, and never again have to chop wood or shovel coal. There she'll be, sitting in her beautiful house, all warm and comfortable, with plenty of everything she needs and not a care in the world.

I always had this dream of being successful. It was planted and nourished deep in my spirit in just the same way as the crops that grew up from the black earth every spring. Grandma's house was surrounded by fields of crops. Every year those fields were prepared and seeded by the farmer's field workers, driving massive tractors and field equipment, plowing and planting with the expectation of a successful harvest. Once the preparation period was complete, the huge planters would come and carefully, in straight rows, plant seeds in the well-prepared soil. The farmer would drive by and watch the bare fields until the rains came and those apparently lifeless seeds, sown in soil that had been prepared months before, came to life.

From that fertile ground sprung up tiny green shoots, each after its own kind. In a few months they'd produce crops so tall that we kids could not see each other when we ran through them.

Every year the farmer with expectations realized his dream, and I watched that farmer's fields of dreams produce a harvest for him. That gave me hope that someday I could produce something within me that could provide an opportunity for my grandmother and me. I had very little knowledge of God at the time, but I saw Him through my grandmother and the way she tirelessly and selflessly cared for all of us. Those fields inspired a dream in me: that I would grow up and become something better for her.

Nevertheless, those around me had demeaning ways of showing that they believed I would never be anything in life, because that's all they could see in me.

"THEY'LL NEVER GROW UP TO BE ANYTHING!"

As I walked home on those long gravel roads, I would hear the folks in the neighborhood sitting on their porches and talking about the disgrace of all seven of us kids burdening this poor widow woman. Or they'd pass us on the street and look towards each other with a kind of unspoken *knowing*, shake their heads, and whisper, "Those bastard kids will never amount to anything."

In school the kids would repeat what they heard their parents say. "You don't even have a daddy. You'll never grow up to be anything!" But those mean words and ugly remarks just drove me to hold onto my dreams even tighter.

My own relatives were no better than the neighbors, and probably worse. My aunts and uncles would make cruel jokes about me. They would stand me up in front of the family during holiday gatherings and make me turn around while they tried to decide if I looked like a particular relative. There was a rumor that my mother had had an affair with one of my uncles, and I was the result.

Because of this ugly rumor about me, some family members did not want me around. They hated me and made sure that I clearly understood that I was rejected. Their harsh words and cruel looks pierced my young soul.

Some folks believe that because you're a small child you either don't understand or won't remember such things. But I understood them all too well. The pain of rejection is never easy to forget or forgive, but they were my family, and I would soon grow to understand the greatest strength of mankind is forgiveness. Nevertheless, these attitudes just drove me farther toward my dream of success. Even at a very early age, I was determined to not let all of their rejection and cruelty defeat me. It only steeled my resolve to succeed in life and become far more than they ever expected.

Someday they would all be shocked and sorry they were so mean. Someday they'd realize how wrong they'd all been about me. Someday, it would all be very different—just wait and see. Someday, they'll thank me for being me...

WALKING IN THE FIELDS OF DREAMS

I grew up walking on dirt roads by cotton, wheat, soybeans, and milo fields all by myself, and just dreaming as I watched the birds, bees, and other animals. Everyone who knew me would tell you, "Oh, that Jerome. He's always walking those fields."

I was a learner, and those fields of dreams became my teachers. I knew every path through those fields and every secret little animal hideout. I knew where the foxholes were located, and I would often get dried bread from my Grandma's kitchen and feed the little baby foxes. It almost seemed as if those foxes knew me, although they never let me get really close. I would lay my ear down on the ground above their holes to hear the little baby foxes inside and I would leave the bread outside for them to come out and find.

I walked those fields by myself, and I dreamed. I became determined to live my life in a different way from what I saw around me. I became determined to do things in life for myself and for others. Each day I became more and more determined to become an instrument to break the curse of bondage and the poverty mentality in my family. I was determined to make my grandmother proud of the sacrifices she made to raise me.

At fourteen years old I became the man of the house. My grandmother's mother died, and Grandma just fell apart. It hurt her very deeply.

Great Grandma, Ida Bell Redd, had given strength to us all. I remember coming home from school every day and walking five miles to her house to make sure she had water, mow the grass, feed the dogs, and clean up for her. She would always reward me with candy or one of her favorite dishes she had prepared. She would often tell me stories of my great-grandfather Andrew Redd, whom everyone, even the white man, feared. She had a Cherokee outfit with lots of feathers in a big truck that had belonged to him, and she often told us how he had liked his steaks and meats just warmed and ninety per-cent raw. I always wished I had known this man of power and fearlessness.

After her death, I stepped forward and became the leader in our household, even though I wasn't the oldest. I chopped cotton every summer and took a variety of odd jobs to earn money to help my grandmother and my sisters and brothers.

That was my childhood; I never really had a lot of fun as a child. Instead, I learned to take on a leadership role in helping my family, and I determined within myself that all of the poverty and bondage in my family would stop once and for all with me.

MEETING GOD IN THOSE FIELDS OF DREAMS

Down there in those fields, all the passion and desire to be different, to do better, was born inside my heart. It came from walking in those fields all alone, dreaming, hoping, and planning. I had no knowledge, no father, no mother, no one to pour himself or herself into me and encourage me. I just had myself and those endless, dusty fields—those fields of dreams—and I had my greatest mentor, Grandma Jessie Mae Redd.

Much later I discovered that someone else had been with me. Someone had walked with me in those fields while I was dreaming. God had been with me. The day would eventually come when I would realize that even those dreams had not come from within me. They had come from Him.

There was nothing I learned or was taught by someone that made me think the way I did. God was calling me to something more, as far back as I remember. Nevertheless, it would be years before I would really know Him. God had a plan for my life, and even while I was living in poverty His plan was unfolding.

The Bible says that when your father and mother forsake you that God will take you up. He Himself will raise you when you're abandoned and alone. And that's what He did. He breathed Himself into my spirit through those dreams. In those fields of dreams, God was planting the seeds of success, hope, and vision for something beyond what I had ever seen or known. It was God Himself who caused me to want to stop that curse of poverty in my life and end the cycle of despair and need.

God showed Himself to me through my grandmother, and through her He taught me to love my oppressor, to hate evil, and to be grateful for the little I had.

LORD, I WANT...

To some extent the vision God placed within my heart for my future was very specific. I remember praying a prayer one night. I was in tears, desperately wanting to get out of those sticks. I just didn't want to live there anymore. I didn't want to continue watching my grandmother suffer, receive food stamps, and have people call her "dumb" because she couldn't read. I got tired of hearing her refer to white boys and girls as "sir" and "ma'am" when they were young enough to be her grandchildren. It had all started to hurt, and for the first time I was becoming deeply angry at this terrible disease called poverty.

I looked up to that great big sky and spoke out loud. "Lord, I want success and a family. I want a wife, and I want three children. I want a girl, and I want two boys." Interestingly, today I have two sons and a daughter. But my request was even more specific than that. I told God that I wanted my daughter to be the oldest, and today my daughter is the oldest of my three children. Many years later, God reminded me of that prayer. After our third child was born, my wife decided that she didn't want to have any more children. At that moment, God gently brought back to my memory my prayer on the porch of Grandma's house. God spoke into my heart, "You told Me that you wanted a girl as the oldest and two sons, remember, on that porch when you were crying and dreaming?"

That moment was so amazing to me. I had spoken something into existence through prayer—it happened exactly as I asked. I learned that God is just as real as you and me. He will give you the desires of your heart. Even when your knowledge of Him is limited, God hears and answers our prayers, and His only desire is for us to do His will in return.

GROWING UP IN HARMONDALE

Growing up on a dirt road in a small town in the segregated South was like going back in time. Harmondale is located at the boot heel of Missouri, right on the state line between Missouri and Arkansas, where the flat terrain stretches on for miles. Our closest neighbor was more than a mile away.

All seven of us, eight with grandma, lived in my grandmother's wooden shack, which consisted of four rooms: a living room, two bedrooms, and a small kitchen. There were two beds in each bedroom. All four girls and my grandmother slept in one bedroom, and the three of us boys in the other. I was the middle child.

I never really felt the full impact of our poverty until I attended high school, because even though we lived in a shack, our neighbors lived in much the same way, and we all kept our homes clean. In my neighborhood, there weren't *haves* and *have-nots*; we all had the same things. We lived on a farm and my uncles and aunts had farms, too. Whenever someone killed a cow or a hog, they would make sure we got some of it.

We could always go over to a relative or neighbor's house and get bacon, sausage, or flour. And there was fishing—everyone fished, and there were lots of fish to catch, so we always had something to eat. We might come home from school and find nothing in the refrigerator but a bottle of water, but when suppertime came my grandmother always served a nice hot meal. She always had a pot of beans or a plate of fried chicken for all of us to eat. My grandmother knew how to make do. She could turn a bag of flour, a pot of water, and a package of beans into a gourmet meal.

High school made me aware of the degree of the poverty in which we lived; there I was with kids who owned cars and dressed in better clothes. They had money and could buy things that I didn't have. They paid for their lunches while most of us got ours free. It was sometimes embarrassing because everyone knew that if you didn't pay for your lunch it was because you were poor. But it only made me more determined to achieve better things. Now my children pay for their lunch.

WHO WAS MY FATHER?

Throughout all of my school years it seemed that the other kids were always talking about their dads. Their dads did this; their dads did that; their dads took them here; their dads went there.

I was a very good basketball player in high school, and my talent would later help our team become the state champions. For our final game on a college campus in Cape Gurado, Missouri, the "Show Me Show Down," the proud fathers were to escort the players onto the floor. The loudspeaker began announcing the players' names and their fathers' names. As they were announced, the fathers walked their sons out onto the floor in front of all the cheering fans.

When my turn came, the announcer said, "Jerome Edmonson, escorted by his grandmother, Miss Jessie Redd."

I was one of the few players without a father, and I felt humiliated. I loved my grandmother with all my heart, but I suddenly felt different from everyone else. I just hated everybody after that game, and I started asking myself hard questions about my father.

It should have been the best game in my life, because my team, the Senath-Hornersville Lions, became state champions, but afterwards, instead of excitement, my mind was filled with questions. What kind of man would just leave his child? What kind of mother would just dump off her kids with their grandmother and take off? I loved my grandmother so much, but my heart was pierced with pain. I wanted to know—I needed to know—who my father was. I began to ask my family members, "Who was my father? What was he like? Why didn't he want me?"

They replied, "Well, they say your mother slept with so-and-so. They say that he is your father."

So there I was, a kid with lots of dreams and aspirations, who just wanted to know his father. I used to dream that one day someone would knock at the door and I would answer it. A tall, well-dressed man would open his arms to me and say, "I'm your father. I've come to take care of you." But that never happened.

Finally, during one of her few visits from New York, I got up the courage to confront my mother with the question. I asked, "Who is my father?"

Defiant and angry, she retorted, "You don't need to know!" And that was it. Even though, I never hated her, and while other family members said bad things about her, I still loved the lady who gave me life.

Nobody messed with my mother because she had so much attitude; she carried a pearl-handled knife and wasn't afraid to use it. She lived her life addicted to alcohol and drugs. But she would still come to visit all of us about once a year, and she might even bring us some clothes or a couple of dollars. Still, we never spent much time with my mother. Once she called to say that if she didn't get out of New York there were people who were going to kill her. What I received from my mother were questions, fears, and turbulence—the phantoms that chased me through life, the fears that challenged me and threatened my dreams. These were the fears that I would need to maximize and overcome in order to realize the success I wanted.

MEMORIES OF MY GRANDMOTHER

My stability and love came from my grandmother. She was kind and loving, and she cared about everybody. She wouldn't even let sick stray dogs suffer. She'd bring these poor animals home, put oil on their coats to rid them of mange or parasites, feed them, and nurse them back to health.

My grandmother cared a great deal about us. She would sit us down and talk to us about becoming successful in life and doing better for ourselves than she had been able to do. She'd say, "Your grandmother don't have an education, but you have to get an education. I had to quit school to take care of my kids, but you children need to get your education. I'm going to do without so you will have."

Grandma was determined that we would not want for things. Even if she had to spend her last dime, she would make sure our needs were met. Her clothes were ragged and her shoes had holes in them, but she always made sure we had clothes and shoes for ourselves.

In those winter months when she chopped wood, the weather would be so frigid that it would bring tears to her eyes. She'd have frozen tears streaking down her face as she sang worship songs and chopped wood. She'd get up early in the morning, go outside, and put wood around the bottom of the water pump. Then she'd pour kerosene on it and start a fire to try and thaw out the frozen pump so that she could bring in water for us to drink and bathe.

My grandmother was our world. Had she not taken us in and raised us with lots of love and discipline, there's no telling where we would be. Honestly, half of us would probably be dead or living out on the streets of New York. God only knows what a nightmare our lives might have been without her.

My grandmother was also the leader of my life, the first example of an entrepreneur. God's Word says, "Train up a child in the way he should go: and when he is old, he will not depart from it" (Prov. 22:6, KJV). The seeds of truth, godliness, and survival she planted into my life grew up in my soul. I have not departed from the entrepreneurial teachings of her life, and I would never depart from her.

While in high school, I had an opportunity to go and live with my uncle, Larry Redd, in Lansing, Michigan. It would have led to an opportunity to play basketball at Michigan State University, which I deeply wanted to do, but I refused to leave my grandmother. Because of my great love for her and the desire to pay her back by becoming successful and taking care of her, I chose to stay down South and go to school there so I could continue to be close to her. Even when I went into the military, I wrote to her constantly and sent money every time I received a check.

My grandmother believed in me. She always told me, "Jerome, I know your going to 'mount to somethin' one day. I know my Jerome is going to be someone special."

GRANDMA'S COOKING

Grandma's cooking...well, it's difficult to find words to describe how unbelievably awesome and tasty her legendary cooking really was. She used to say, "Jerome, you come on in here. You listen to me, and come on in here and let me show you how to cook, because one day you will have to take care of yourself and not depend on someone else to cook for you.

Today, I'm in the restaurant industry; that's where I found success. But even that success was first developed as a seed inside my soul. As I watched my grandmother prepare meals, I learned about food, cooking, and what tastes good. Watching her ignited a passion in me to serve quality food that would give pleasure to those who ate it.

Today, I can cook anything. I can bake a cake from scratch, and I can prepare a sweet potato pie that will make your mouth water. People in the restaurant industry, and even my wife, have commented on my skill. They've asked, "Where did you learn how to do all this stuff?"

I watched my grandmother make everything from scratch. I learned from what she did: what ingredients to select, how much to use of each one, and how to blend them together to make it all work. Most importantly, I witnessed the pleasure that cooking and baking gave her.

At sixteen years of age, I could cook four-course meals. I was able to prepare greens, pork chops, cornbread, cakes—the whole nine yards. Often at Christmas, our guests marveled at the foods we prepared, but those delicious meals had simple beginnings. It all goes back to those days on that little dirt road in the middle of nowhere in Missouri where, despite the lack of conveniences such as processed foods and precooked, prepackaged, premeasured ingredients, Grandma worked tirelessly to prepare us wonderful, tasty, healthful meals.

MY PROMISES TO GRANDMA

Once, when Grandma got very sick and was forced to reckon with her own mortality, she made me come in and sit down beside her bed. She made me make two promises that became foundational success keys in my life.

Grandma told me, "There's two things that I want you to always do, no matter what condition your life is in. I don't care if you go out and get drunk. I don't care if you're mad at somebody. Just promise me that you will never, ever lay your head down at night without praying. Never go to bed and never close your eyes without thanking God for the day. Promise me you'll never forget to do that."

I asked her why, and she said, "Because tomorrow is not promised to you, and life, no matter how you choose to live it, is a gift from God. So, whether you choose to live it for Him or recklessly for yourself, always thank the sustainer of your life, and one day you will become what He birthed you to be. Not doing His will, my dear grandson, is the only thing in life that God will judge you for. So no matter what condition you're in, physically or mentally, pray."

I said, "Grandma, I promise you that I'll never forget to do that."

From that day forward I have never neglected to lay my head down in prayer before going to sleep. Even if I forget as I'm going to bed, I'm unable to fall asleep until I remember to pray.

Grandma continued, "This is the second thing I want you to do...I've lived my life not having, but so many people have given. Always remember that when somebody gives you something—I don't care if it's ten years down the line..." She used a watermelon as an example and said, "If someone gives you a watermelon, even if you can't pay them back for ten years, when you are finally in a position to pay them back, find that person, search him out, and give him back more than he gave you. In that way, you'll show him that you appreciate what he did. From this you will learn it's better to be a giver than a receiver."

Then Grandma took my hand, looked me right in the eye, and said, "Never take kindness for granted, son, because people don't have to help you. If they choose to help you, then you write it down in your heart. The person who helped you must benefit from what you became as a result of that gift."

Later on in my life, I began to understand more about the biblical principles of giving and receiving. Nevertheless, those principles were first seeded into my heart by my precious Grandma, whose wisdom has lit a pathway for me in life—a pathway that took me from being an abandoned child in those fields of dreams to having prosperity and success in every aspect of life. Grandma had great seeds of wisdom.

THE MOURNER'S BENCH

During a revival meeting one hot summer evening, while we sat fanning ourselves in our little country church, Grandma leaned over to me on the pew and declared, "It's time for you to be saved, Jerome!"

I had been snickering and whispering to my best friend, Willie Nelson, and waiting patiently until church was over so that we could run outside and play. "Saved, Grandma?" It hadn't occurred to me that I needed saving, except maybe from the heat and those long sermons.

"Yes, boy, saved!" she declared, with the look on her face that told me I'd better not argue. She knew what was best.

Grandma yanked me up from the bench and walked me to the front of our little church. Now, in a Baptist church in the South, we had to sit on what we called a *mourning bench* when we were seeking salvation. Grandma plunked my skinny frame down on that hard bench.

Willie's mother decided that the day of salvation had come for his young soul, too. Plunk, Willie was placed on the mourning bench beside me.

So, here we were, my best friend, Willie Nelson, and a whole bunch of other people, all lined up on that hard mourning bench in the front of the church. We were all waiting there for salvation.

Every night somebody would come off that bench and go down front for salvation. The pastor would be preaching and spitting. "You feel the Lord! You feel it! Come on down front here if you feel it! Come on to Jesus!"

And all of a sudden, one person or another would jump up and scream and run down front to get saved.

At the end of the night, Willie and I would go up to one of the newly saved souls and ask, "What did you feel?"

They would say, "I don't know. I just felt something...I just felt it."

The next night would come and more people would jump up off that mourning bench. Willie and I kept asking them what had happened. "Man, come on, tell us what we need to feel so we can come off that bench."

Finally, on Thursday, the fourth night of the revival, Willie and I were the only two people left on the mourning bench. We realized that if we didn't jump up off that bench pretty soon, we were going to be preached at all the way until Sunday.

Then, halfway into the sermon, Willie jumped up off the bench.

Now, I was greatly relieved. I thought, *I know I'm going to find out what I need to feel, because that's my boy. Willie's going to let me in on it!* As we were walking home down the dirt gravel road in the darkness, I asked, "So, Willie, do I have to ask you? What did you feel?"

He rubbed his bottom and smiled widely, the way that only Willie could smile, and said, "Jerome, listen, I didn't feel nothing. I was on that mourning bench for four nights, and my butt hurts. I just had to come off it."

So the next night I came off that bench, too. We got saved all right. We got saved from that hard wooden bench and sore butts—and that's about all we got saved from!

GOD AND GRANDMA

My grandmother wanted me to develop a strong faith and a close relationship with Jesus Christ. She talked about God constantly. She always told me that no matter what happened in my life, "God will make a way. Jerome, don't forget, God will make a way for you."

So my grandmother was my father. She was the man of my life; she was my inspiration. She was everything that a kid could want in one person. I really didn't miss having a father in the home because of the caring and nurturing I received from Grandma. She provided all the fathering I needed. Jessie Mae Redd, my grandma, birthed an entrepreneur's spirit in me that would later manifest itself in my life.

GRANDMA'S FOOD STAMPS

Grandma couldn't write, so she would take me with her when she went into the next town to pick up her food stamps. I would help her sign for them, and then we'd shop together in town. I'll never forget the time a very prideful young white girl shamed my grandmother for not being able to write.

We were waiting to receive the foodstamps when this snippy blonde woman handed Grandma a pen and ledger. Grandma took the pen in her hand and slowly held it up, faltering in her movements.

The young woman placed her hand on her hips and snapped, "Come on, woman! Won't you hurry up? Can't you write?"

Softly, my grandmother said, "Yes, ma'am. I'll be there. Yes, ma'am. I'll be finished in a minute..."

Now, here's this snippy young girl, and here's my grandmother with all this wisdom, the pride of my life. This spoiled brat of a girl who wasn't much older than myself was completely humiliating my grandmother. I hated that lady.

Many years later, I had the chance to return to that little office. My Uncle Bill and I had come back to take my Grandma out of poverty. I would be caring for her from now on.

So, when I arrived in Kennett, Missouri, you know what? That woman was still there. For years I had burned inside with hatred for that woman who had humiliated my precious grandmother.

When I saw that woman once again, I thought, *Oh my goodness. Now is my chance.*

I walked up to her and told her that my grandmother would not be needing food stamps any longer. Then I said, "You may not remember me, but I grew up down here. I came in here one day a long time ago, when you were very young. My grandmother was standing in line, and you told her to hurry up and sign. You said, 'What is it woman, you don't know how to write?' You may not have realized it, but you humiliated my sweet grandmother, and it was one of the most hurtful things that ever happened in my life."

She put her now-aging hands on her hips and declared, "Well, they still like that. They still can't write."

I said, "Well, I've lived a lifetime just to come to tell you one thing."

She said, "What?"

I said, "You can take these food stamps and this check and you can shove them..." I won't repeat the rest of what I said.

Then I continued, "I'm taking my grandmother out of here, and she will never need government assistance again, because I'm a successful businessman and I'm going to take care of her for the rest of her life."

I balled the paper up, threw it at her, and walked out.

It felt so good to do that. I felt like I was on top of the world. I had come back and accomplished what I always said I would. I was taking care of Grandma.

On the way back to the car, my uncle stopped me and said I should go back and apologize. I went back in the following day.

"Ma'am, yesterday I was angry over something that happened years ago, and I finally got the frustration out. I want to let you know that I apologize for my actions yesterday. It was pain from years ago that caused me to say what I said. However, what I really wanted to tell you is that God has blessed me. I'm a blessed man, and my grandmother doesn't need government assistance anymore. I'm going to take care of her the rest of her life. She raised me in these woods, and she sacrificed everything so that I could have a chance in life. Now, it's time for me to take care of her. I appreciate all that has been done over the years to help her and others like her, but from here on out I'm going to take care of her. So, God bless you all."

Before I left, I added, "Try to find it in your spirit to treat people with more respect and with greater kindness, like I'm doing right now. You might even consider apologizing for hurtful things you've said in the past. If you can do that, you'll find that life will treat you very well. You'll grow and you'll prosper, and you won't have a lot of past regrets to live with as you get on in years."

And she said, "Thank you, son."

GROW YOUR OWN FIELD OF DREAMS

There are those who say that dreams are empty and meaningless—that any poor, suffering child can ride away from his misery on the back of a dream. But I'm sharing my story with you because I want you to know that dreams can come true. Every dream that you have within your heart holds the seed of potential. And when that potential is watered and nourished with faith and hope, dreams can take root and grow up like cottonseeds planted in a well-prepared field. God can grow your seeds of potential into fields of dreams. He did just that for me.

CHAPTER 2

MAXIMIZING THE GENERATIONAL CURSE OF FAILURE

Before I could realize my dreams, I had a lot to overcome. One of the first hurdles in my life was failure. As African-American farm workers living in the Deep South, failure was expected of us. It was sown into the fiber of our souls by low expectations, demeaning attitudes, and condescending words.

For the most part, everyone around us farmed the land, growing cotton, soybeans, and corn. African-Americans formed the workforce, just as they had since the first fields were cleared and plowed. We were field hands and farmers who rarely owned the land on which we labored. In the hot summers we sweated in the unrelenting sun chopping cotton, and in the cold springs and falls we plowed, cleared the land, and seeded it for the next season of crops.

Not much had changed in nearly two hundred years of cotton farming in Harmondale, Missouri. In the fields, it was, "Yes, sir" and "No, sir."

Field hands and their families did what they were told, and they didn't make suggestions. The best you could do in Harmondale was keep your head down, stay out of trouble, and spend the weekends drinking away the monotony and boredom of your life's low expectations.

These men were my role models, but much of what they were teaching me was what had been seeded into them: low expectations. They were a community of men groomed by low expectations and failure. These seeds had been ingested into their spirits along with their mother's milk. Failure was the harvest of their lives.

Although they might have wonderful ideas and make keen observations while we were alone, when the farmer or the guy in charge showed up, these men responded as they had been programmed. They never did the things they spoke about to each other, and so they never grew. They never saw a way to move beyond "yes, sir" and "no, sir." Their responsibility was to take care of the farmer's fields, and then just go home and get a nice bottle of liquor. It became the sum total of their existence.

All the men in my town chopped cotton in the fields, drove a tractor, or drove a truck. What's the success of a farm hand versus that of a farmer? You work the fields, but you don't own them. You drive the equipment, but you don't buy it. You never own the store—you just make your purchases there. The limited resources you had, the strength, knowledge, skill, were used to benefit someone else. That was simply what was expected. No one seemed to expect any more. This truth still permeates our modern-day society.

I was being programmed, too. I began to believe that I would never be anything more than a field hand. I thought, *I'll farm, get a little wooden house like everyone else's, and maybe meet a girl, get married, and raise a family*. Mr. Niland's field was the largest in the region, and I thought that if I could work on his farm, I would be successful. So, at fifteen, I began to chop cotton.

This programming was enduring and pervaded the attitudes and beliefs that we all shared—everybody's low expectations. They made us believe that we were nobody.

"You guys are workers; you're field hands." That's the way everyone acted, and that's the message that was communicated to us.

That's why a lot of folks never made it out of that environment: they were programmed to fail and became dependent on the very thing that robbed them of their true potential. I see the same kind of programming in the way corporate America treats its workforce. Workers are given a little bonus here, a little pat on the back there. They live their lives believing there are positions up at the top to which they might ascend. Nevertheless, over the long term, most of those individuals will never rise above a certain level.

One of the biggest diseases of poverty is paycheck dependency. It makes people behave like the children of Israel after God freed them from bondage and captivity—in the midst of the wilderness experience they wanted to return to captivity. In captivity you know what to expect and there is little requirement to exert yourself by using your own gifts and talents. I call this the plantation mentality, and it has enslaved vast numbers of people in corporate America today.

Many of the workers who have bought into the plantation mentality eventually find that one day, for no reason at all, they've been terminated or laid off and robbed of their dreams. They traded a willingness to remain dependent for security, and they never stepped out into entrepreneurial empowerment.

Being an employee requires submission and a willingness to be controlled. You don't have to live in the Deep South to be programmed for failure. A mountain of low expectations and programmed failure stands between most of us and success. Therefore, understanding and scaling this mountain is vital in order to achieve the success that is your destiny and birthright.

When I got my first job chopping cotton I was very proud. I thought that I had grown up now that I was one of the working men. The farmer would come and pick us up, we'd all pile into the back of his truck, and he'd take us out to the fields. I would work hard out in the field all day, and at night I'd come home and sit with the light on in the kitchen, a sheet pulled over the doorway, holding a BB gun. I'd get bread, put it in the top of a bottle, and place it beside a cabinet. Then I'd sit there and shoot field mice—when they came out to eat that bread I'd pop them. Sometimes they'd get away, and I'd have to go behind the stove to kill them. There would be blood everywhere, and I'd clean it up. I'd kill fifteen or twenty every night, but there always seemed to be more of them. I would do this every night until I fell asleep.

Even though I had a job and I was making a living, we weren't living. We were still in the same conditions.

Nevertheless, I was proud of being a working man. I was making a living, I was doing something for myself, and I was helping take care of Grandma. I was helping make ends meet. Jerome was growing up; it was my first step into maturity. People began treating me better because I had a job, and I was able to buy a few things for myself.

Still, when I prayed at night and when I dreamed, I knew there was something missing. I didn't have Scripture passages memorized, and I didn't even own a Bible growing up. But I had such a belief in the Creator of that star, in the Creator of that dream. I just knew that He wanted more for me.

That's why I spent so much time with Him—my grandmother taught me to pray to Him, and I just knew that this God would deliver me. God was the one who put the feeling of purpose and potential in me, and I knew that I was living far below what He desired for me.

DEPROGRAMMING MYSELF

In order to succeed in your life you must face the failure that's been programmed into your spirit.

I had to deprogram myself. You see, my identity had been tempered with the low expectations I received. I needed to discover who I really was—not in the eyes of those around me, but in the eyes of God. Discovering my true identity was a gift—a gift that gave me the definition necessary to achieve success. Self-discovery is the first key to success, because if you don't know who you are, you will never be able to help anyone else. Identity is what opportunity demands.

I developed faith in those fields of dreams, faith to look for something more than what I saw all around me. I grew up dreaming that I could be more and have more. I looked at that star every night and it gave me hope that God had a vision for me. My Creator had a destiny in mind for me that offered far more than the narrow definition I received in Harmondale.

One night I lay on my back with my arms under my head and prayed. *Lord, I know you're up there looking down at me. I don't want to stay here in Harmondale. I want to go to the big city. I want to stretch out and find the life that I know you have for me out there somewhere.*

I'm tired of chopping cotton. I'm tired of being called names. I'm tired of that boss throwing his hoe at me and telling me to hurry up. God, take me to my destiny. Take me far away from here.

Facing the programming of my life was anything but easy. I left those fields of Harmondale as a young man and went to live with my successful uncle.

MAXIMIZING THE POWER OF FEAR

Far too many Americans are satisfied with dependency. We grow up believing that the government will take care of us, and that's why so many people were terrified on September 11th. What would happen to us if there was no government to hold our hands and help us?

It's time to look beyond the confines of our narrowly defined expectations and take control of our destinies. Many of us are born with great intelligence, talent, insight, and creativity. Yet these seeds of greatness are buried in our coffins when we die. We allow the light within us to die long before.

In order to realize success, we must reject failure, which involves rejecting the low expectations and limited definitions that others have given us, especially in the workplace.

PROGRAMMED DEPENDENCY

Many of us are programmed to fail by our surroundings, our associations, and the unwise counsel we receive throughout our lives. In addition, few of us look closely at our lifestyles and the people with whom we surround ourselves. Yet what we listen to, what goes into our ears, also goes into our psyche, where it has the power to determine who we become. When our lives are surrounded by negativity we won't grow.

There's really only one key to being deprogrammed. It involves rediscovering yourself in the light of truth—in the light of Yeshua Ha Maschia, Jesus the Christ. That's the only way to get out of the mold. You must realize that people and environments that don't really know you have defined you. Self-discovery is the key to success at anything you want to do in life. Nothing is impossible for the man or woman who knows who they were created to become. You must receive your definition from your Creator, Jesus Christ. That's what was happening to me every night as I looked into that great big sky. It caused me to take the limits off of myself.

You can be successful in the workplace, but God has to lead you in that environment, so you have to develop a solid relationship with your Creator. It doesn't matter how you were brought up. People may look at me today and think that my life has always been easy. But it hasn't been. I didn't have anything to start out with—no parents, no money, no opportunities. However, I did have vision in the form of dreams that were planted into my heart by God. I let my faith take me to the realization of my dreams. I had faith in what I did not know.

You may be fatherless or homeless. You may be addicted to crack cocaine or in prison and feel that you have no way out. But that doesn't mean you're a failure. Make up your mind that you will not be defined by your circumstances. Find your definition, your true identity in your Creator. Your inability to become who God has called you to be affects other people. There's a world around you waiting for you to step up to the plate and take your position so that they can take theirs, too.

Find out who you really are, and reject the limitations of your environment, and you'll succeed just as I did. If I can do it, so can you.

LIVING BEYOND THE DEFINITIONS OF OTHERS

Success is nothing more than understanding God's perfect will for your life and doing it—doing those things you were set on this earth to do. Success for each one of us is different because we are all called to do different things. That's why I graduated from a people-centered life a long time ago. People will destroy you with their own ideas of who you are. Some will even hate your success and waste their energy criticizing everything you do.

Therefore, finding your purpose will take some amount of solitude. You've got to pull away from other people a little. I did that as a youngster as I walked those fields of dreams. Beware, because who you associate with and to whom you listen will eventually define you. The law of association says you will become the top five people you associate with the most. Don't kid yourself by telling yourself that what you listen to won't shape your behavior. It will. The words and expectations of others will have an effect upon you. You must begin to control that stream of input into your soul. The garbage you allow into your psyche will shape the way you think.

If the people you associate with think you'll never achieve anything, then get away from them and surround yourself with people who think more highly of you. Associate with achievers and you'll become one of them.

If you don't know what you're called to do, then get off by yourself until you do. Get away from the pull of everyone around you and think about you. What do you want? What makes you excited? Get in touch with your passions, purposes, and desires.

Sometimes, I get away from everybody just to go and think. I get on a plane and tell my wife, "I'll be back in a few days." She knows that I need to clear my own head, to get away and think.

Identity can only come from deep inside of you. Nobody, no matter how well intentioned he or she is or how much he or she loves you, can give that to you. It can only come from inside of you, and from a relationship with the One who created you.

So make a decision to become who you were intended to be today, and begin to affect the lives of others tomorrow. You don't need to be president. You don't need to be prime minister. You just need to fully and completely become who you really are, who God meant for you to be.

Breaking the Generational Curse

If you live your life in ignorance about your true destiny and potential as a man or woman, then you will continue to raise a generation of children with low expectations. What you expect of your life and the lives of your children will determine what they grow up to become. If you know nothing and teach them what you know, what do you think they will become? Nothing! Because that's exactly what you've taught them. So now you have another generation of ignorance that knows absolutely nothing about their true inheritance and purpose.

Nothing. That's what happens when people live outside of God's presence, because everything outside of God is nothingness. Now, you may have money and lots of it. Look at some of the athletes, celebrities, and business leaders who have received national acclaim but do not have a relationship with God. Such individuals may know the game. Nevertheless, did you realize that the majority of all athletes end up after their illustrious careers without a job? Even when their careers net millions, they can wind up broke and needy.

Such people were programmed from the beginning to fail, and despite several years of success, they still end up with failure. Even with an opportunity for genuine success and prosperity, they never truly break free from their failure mentality. The failure that defined them as children catches up with them as they get older.

Yet, take a look at those who broke free from the curse of previous generations. Look at the lives of other athletes, businessmen, singers, and other individuals who may have started out with less but ended up with success. Often, they are people who have given their lives to Kingdom living and allowed their Creator to give them their true identity. They've been reprogrammed with truth; therefore, the curse has been broken. Be ye transformed from poverty by the renewing of your mind.

SETTING A STANDARD OF IDENTITY

One of the people who really helped me lay a hold of better expectations for my life was my Uncle Bill. When I was a kid, Uncle Bill would periodically come down from Michigan to visit with us. Although we never had the luxury of a telephone, everyone seemed to know when he was in town.

He would drive into that dusty community in a shiny new Cadillac, and every head would turn in his direction. He became a role model for me. When he came, everybody would gather around him. He had money, cars, and lots of prestige. He didn't depend on anyone, and everyone loved him. He was a giver and always left a blessing behind whenever he came. I always wanted to be just like him when I grew up.

With my limited knowledge of God, I would look up into those starry Missouri nights and talk to God about Uncle Bill and how I wanted to be just like him. I would say, *Now, God, I want to go to where Uncle Bill is and become successful in life just like he is.* He set a standard in my life and became my goal.

If you never set standards and goals and never make a plan for your life, then the road ahead will take you nowhere. Uncle Bill was my standard, my vision, and my goal as a child. He also was the father that I never had. He would grab me around the neck and say, "I'm going to be your daddy, boy, and you don't have to worry about a father."

That felt so good to me because now I had a successful father. Uncle Bill had integrity and demanded it from everyone. Wherever we went together he'd introduce me as his son, and people would say I looked just like him.

After I began praying to God to become like Uncle Bill, my grades at school started to improve. I began to plan to finish high school and attend college. I started to see myself driving a shiny new car like my uncle's and working at an important job like his. Even though these were material things, they were birthing in me a desire to be greater than I was, greater than what people around me expected.

I wanted to become a *have* not a *have-not* so I could take care of my grandmother. I became driven by a desire to have what Uncle Bill had and to go where he went. He would tell me, "I used to live here, boy, and I went up North and got me a good job and became someone."

So as a young teenager I decided that I would finish school, go up North like my uncle, and get a good job. Eventually, I would come back and take my grandmother up there. That became my driving passion—and that passion had enough power to help me to break free from the power of generational curses.

REACHING HIGHER

As I meditated upon my goal of leaving Missouri and getting a good job, I increasingly began to reject the negative programming I had received. I rejected my environment along with its low expectations. I told my grandmother that I no longer wanted to chop cotton like my family had done before me. I wanted more from my life than that.

She said, "Well son, what are you going to do?"

I said, "Grandma, I'm going to play basketball."

And she said, "Well, where will you learn to play basketball?" Grandma couldn't afford a basketball court, so it seemed there was no way I could practice and achieve my desire.

At about that same time, a storm blew through our little town and high winds knocked down a big electricity pole. When I discovered that pole lying on the road, I went home and got a chain, wrapped it around the pole, and dragged it home. It took me all day to get that pole home. When I finally got it there, I cut it in half with a handsaw. I dug a deep hole at the end of our little dirt road and tried to lift the pole into the hole.

It was impossible. The more I tried the more frustrated I became. Finally, one of the farmers asked me what I was doing with the pole. When I shared my dream he decided to help, and he came by with a tractor to lift the pole into place. What a prize! The pole was upright and sturdy.

Now, all I needed to do was to make a backdrop. I nailed a piece of plywood to the pole, then added a rim made out of the spokes of an old bicycle wheel. I straightened it up and hammered pieces on the side, and now I had my own basketball court in front of my house. I was on my way to realizing my dream.

Everyday before and after school I used my new basketball hoop to perfect my game. And now those fields of dreams became my gymnasium. The same fields that I used to walk and dream in became my track, and I ran in them every day to get into shape. I worked on my dream of leaving Missouri and becoming successful every day of my life. I really didn't understand it at the time, but my dreams were rising to the next level of success. They were becoming a plan.

DREAMING, DESTINY, AND DETERMINATION

Finally, I was in the seventh grade and the day for basketball tryouts came. I tried out but didn't make the team. When I learned that the tryout results had been posted I ran out to the wall where the names were listed. I left feeling like the saddest person in the universe because my name wasn't on the list.

Nevertheless, I didn't throw away my dream. I went home and ran on my track even more, and I shot more baskets. The next thing I knew I was sprouting—it seemed I was growing taller every week. Suddenly this skinny little kid started looking more like a man. Everyone started to comment, "Look at Jerome; he's getting tall."

The following year a much taller Jerome tried out again. The next day I went once again very slowly to that same wall, and when I saw my name on the list I yelled, "Yes!" Finally, I had made the team. But I didn't stop trying to improve myself. I kept working, running, shooting, and practicing until I became the best player on that team.

That same year, I spent the summer in Lansing, Michigan, with my Uncle Larry, where I got an opportunity to meet Magic Johnson. My uncle was his communications teacher. I went over to a table where my uncle was sitting and teaching, and there he was: one of the greatest basketball players in the NBA. I was totally speechless: *Oh my God. It's Magic J...J....*

I sat down at the table and my uncle looked at me and said, "What's wrong?"

I said, "That's Magic Johnson."

"Well, Jerome, I'm Magic's communications teacher. I'm working with him on some of his commercials." Then Magic said, "Let me finish, and when I'm done I'll shoot some hoops with you outside." I couldn't believe it—me and Magic one-on-one!

Following the session with my uncle, Magic did what he promised. I told him, "You know, I want to be a good basketball player just like you."

He said, "Jerome, if you have a passion, and you have a dream to play basketball like me, you do it." Holding the ball in his hands he looked into my eyes. "This was my dream, but don't do it like I did; do it even better." Well, I knew all about dreaming. I had planted fields of dreams in that little town in Missouri.

And now, Magic Johnson was standing in front of me telling me that if I had a dream, I could achieve it. I thought, "Wow!" Suddenly, my expectations had all changed. My dream was possible, and Magic was my inspiration.

The next year was my freshman year and the coach asked me to play varsity on the high school team. Now, my dream was getting increasingly real. I was a big shot, a ninth grader playing varsity basketball on the starting line-up. The word floating in our little impoverished community down South was that Jerome was going to make it. He was named in all the newspaper articles as one of the best.

I'M GOING TO MAKE IT

I practiced more and more, and I expected basketball to help me to become a success, to help me to care for my grandmother, leave the Deep South, and drive fancy cars. Uncle Bill had achieved success as a master chef in Michigan, and I was going to do the same thing through basketball. I put everything into it—my passion, my heart, and my plan. My dreams were now wrapped in a brown leather ball and bouncing up and down a court.

I prayed, *Lord, give me the strength to play this game.* I spent my high school career as a popular basketball player, and I graduated as a high school All-American with scholarships to play ball at local colleges. Nevertheless, I passed up the opportunity to attend several more prestigious colleges in order to remain as close to my grandmother as possible. I ended up going to Mississippi County Community College.

REACHING FOR THE STARS

My life did get better, but in order for that to happen I had to reject the failure programming I received through my environment. I rejected poverty, hardship, low expectations—the curse of generations—and I chose to reach for something better.

The poverty mentality and low expectations of growing up in the Deep South were rooted very deeply in my soul. My limited view of success came from books, conversations, and television. My understanding of success had been passed down through cultural, institutional, religious, and family traditions. In order for me to accurately understand what success was, I had to begin to understand what it was not.

Success was not just an accumulation of the things I desired because I didn't have anything. Yet I knew that if I could look up and see a million stars, then one of them could be my own. And in a universe so large, there had to be a bigger place for a fatherless country boy named Jerome. There was, but getting there required a process of learning, believing, pursuing my dream, and staying with it.

I call this process of holding on to your dream and walking it out step-by-step "tenacity." Developing the tenacity to stay with my dream and to keep believing in it taught me a lot. If you can learn from my struggles, pains, and misfortunes, then perhaps you can bypass some of your own, which is why I've written this book.

But first and foremost you must stop being afraid to dream. The higher you reach, the greater your success. So start on your path to success by determining to dream big and by daring to reach for the stars.

CHAPTER 3

MAXIMIZING THE POWER OF FEAR

As a youngster growing up alone and walking those fields of dreams, I felt like I was my own man. But in order to truly become a man, I had to dig deep inside of me, which is what I was doing as I walked. I lived in those fields and I understood every aspect of them.

I walked those fields and talked to myself—a lot. It was a method of self-discovery, maturing, and soul-searching that for me took the place of having a father. I had to find answers for my life deep inside myself. I wasn't able to look up to a father role model; instead, I had Grandma, my six siblings, and myself. As I walked those fields, I talked to God—a God whom I really hadn't grown to know—and I declared my future.

I would walk and say, *I don't want to live on these dirt roads forever. I don't want my grandmother to suffer.*

Walking those fields helped me to handle the environment in which I lived. I learned to turn over to God those things that troubled my soul. I would say, *Lord, my sister is pregnant. Lord, I don't want my brother to go to jail.* I found answers, faith, comfort, and God in those fields.

A MIRACLE

Once I got into more trouble than I knew how to get out of, and I ran away for a couple of days to those fields. I'm sure that everyone knew where I was, for I was known for walking in those fields. One night, when everyone was looking for me, I decided that I was going to sleep in one of those fields. Late at night, after it had gotten very dark, I started to get pretty scared. As I lay there, a wolf came up and sat right in front of me. At first I thought it was going to eat me, but it just sat there looking at me. Perhaps it had smelled my scent often enough as I walked those fields that it had grown to accept me as a part of the place.

I stared at it for a long time, and then I began to talk to that wolf. *You know, nobody understands me. People think I'm weird, but someday I'm going to move my grandmother out of here. What do you have to worry about? You run around here catching rabbits. There's probably a whole bunch of you out here, and if you wanted to you could probably kill me right now.*

I sat there for a long time talking to the wolf, sharing my life with him, telling him about my dreams. Even though he couldn't understand me, he seemed to be patiently listening. I asked him, *How do you survive? How do you know that you're loved? How do you know when you're happy? How content are you?*

Most people would think that was crazy. But that's what those fields were about to me: learning about birds by watching them, learning about the trees, and learning about the other animals. I might sit for an entire day and watch a bird building its nest, and then I'd go back the next day and watch it complete the job. I'd watch that same bird as it laid its eggs, sat on those eggs, and fluttered about as they hatched. I'd watch it get worms for its young, and sometimes I'd even dig the worms out of the ground and leave them nearby so that it could find them for its young.

There was so much life in those fields, and all the animals held within themselves an instinctive kind of wisdom that let them achieve success. Butterflies, bees, frogs, fish, turtles, and rabbits—none of these creatures seemed to have the worries that I had, and they all seemed to have an ability to succeed at their purpose.

Those fields teemed with life of various kinds—all shapes and sizes. I thought that there had to be a God who was making me live just as He was making all of these animals and plants live. Although I didn't really realize it at the time, God Himself was teaching me. He was walking with me in those fields as a Father, showing me the things that He had created and teaching me principles of truth regarding His creation.

God was telling me to look at the birds of the air and the animals of the field. None of them worry about what tomorrow will bring or how they will eat. Why? Because they trust their Creator to provide all of their needs in each season of their lives.

I saw how these little animals all seemed to know how to nurture their young. The birds took care of their chicks, fed them, and taught them to fly. The foxes and rabbits taught their young too, and so did all of the creatures in God's creation.

It made me wonder why we don't take care of our young like that. Why do we throw our children out and not care for them? Why do we abandon our children, and why did my mother dump me? Why couldn't my mother take care of me as this little bird cared for her young? Why couldn't my mother run and play with me as this rabbit ran and played with its young? Why did my father leave me when this father bird went out and got food for his young and brought it back to feed them? Why didn't my own father provide for me like that?

People thought I was crazy to spend so much time out in those fields. But I was learning a great deal about life there. I'd bring my homework out into those fields and write my papers on my observations of life there. And I'd ask God about what was going to happen in my own life. God listened to me every time I spoke, and He heard every question I asked. I began to understand that God had a plan for my life. It was in those fields that I began to receive God's wisdom for my life, wisdom that I needed to understand throughout my life in order to succeed.

GOD HEARD ME

It's important to understand that God heard me when I asked Him questions. He was filling my heart with questions and feelings that would lead me to His ultimate plan for my life. Those fields were my classroom and I matured as I walked in them, and God was my teacher and mentor.

OVERFLOWING WITH FOOD

As I matured, I started to realize that those fields were teeming with food that could become a revenue stream into my young life. The river would often overflow into the fields, and one day I found hundreds of fish flopping around on the ground after the waters had flooded the land and then receded.

I went home, got my boots, waded out into the mud, and brought home a big sack filled with buffalo and carp fish. Before long, I was selling those fish for a dollar a piece. Eventually, I strung a net in the field drain ditch that ran under the road, so that when the water began to run back to the levy the net would catch the fish. That way, I could continue selling them even when the riverbanks were not overflowing.

Every day, I would hurry home from school and go to the muddy riverbanks to check my nets. They would be full of fish that I could sell to create income for our family. So I was learning a different way to look at what most people down South saw as a constant problem of flooded roads and muddy fields. I saw beyond what they saw, so I took nature's opportunities and turned them into a resource for business opportunities. I maximized my limited opportunities in order to earn an income.

Knowledge Is Not Power—Applied Knowledge Is Power!

You can gain all the knowledge in the world, but all you will have is information unless you apply it. In my own limited way, I was seeking God for wisdom. I needed explanations for my life, and I longed to acquire an understanding that would help me to make sense of my life so I could survive its difficulties.

Success is all about what you understand. As I mentioned in the previous chapter, you must come to an understanding of yourself—it's called self-discovery. The first kingdom principle that unlocks success in life on Earth is driven by your ability to know yourself. You've got to know who you are and what you want in order to be successful.

If you discover everything that is within you—if you are able to unlock the God-given talents and abilities that reside inside you—then there is nothing in the business world that you won't be able to do. You will make happen whatever is put before you.

Knowledge is the key to success. It starts with self-knowledge, but does not by any means stop there. I'll never forget how I reacted when I met Dr. Myles Munroe. I wanted to be like this man. I wanted to teach like him and know everything he knew. It wasn't his position as a preacher that I admired. It was his knowledge and his ability to apply it. He exuded a confidence in himself that was derived from self-discovery. In addition, he could take that knowledge into any environment, including the religious world, the business world, parliament, and even the political arena.

Success is neither magical nor mysterious; it is the natural consequence of consistently applying God's basic fundamentals, called principles, to your life. That's what success is all about.

Hosea 4:6 says, "My people are destroyed for lack of knowledge." Now, you can't stop there when reading this particular Scripture passage, because it goes on to tell you why this occurred. You see, God's people weren't destroyed because knowledge wasn't available to them. The passage continues, "...Because you have rejected knowledge, I also reject you as My priests" (NAS).

How do you reject knowledge? It starts with rejecting self-knowledge. Success begins with understanding your own motives. You must search your own heart in the cold light of day. What is your motive for wanting to become successful? Is it centered on lifestyle and appearance? Do you want to dress like a certain leader or drive a car like a certain businesswoman?

If these are your motives, then your desire for success is false, because you are attempting to pursue another individual's vision instead of your own. If you and I are totally alike then one of us is unnecessary, because God created both of us to be different.

You should never desire to be like someone else or have what someone else has. That's called coveting. God says that His people are destroyed because they lack knowledge—they don't know who they are and why they were created. You've heard it said that "it's not what you know but who you know." I'd take that a step further and say that it's not what you know but what you don't know that's causing your failure, divorce, poverty, and total destruction. It's because you don't know you!

What you don't know is destroying you right now. When I teach I get very personal. This is not philosophy, but real stuff. It's what you need to know to get where you want to go. You can pride yourself in knowing all about the world of business and still perish for lack of knowledge because you don't know you. Success is inevitable if you work diligently to pursue a vision. However, it becomes temporal if you've failed to discover the "you" who must sustain that success.

LEARNING THE LANGUAGE OF BUSINESS

If you moved to a foreign country, you would have to learn the language in order to succeed there. The world of business is no different. The second principle of business success is learning the language.

You can't walk into the business world speaking as you would at church. Business has a totally different language. To succeed in this arena you must understand assets, debt-to-equity ratios, liabilities, cash flow projections, performances, and profits and losses. You must understand income statements and balance sheets. If you can't speak the language of a culture, how are you going to communicate with the citizens of that country?

Therefore, make up your mind to learn what you need to know to succeed. As I walked those fields growing up, God was teaching me His principles from nature. As with Job, God was showing me His greatness through nature, and He was teaching me about right and wrong. He was imparting into my life the wisdom I needed to succeed. I realized that His wisdom had been imparted into the lives of all of His creatures and into nature in general. If they could learn His wisdom for success, so could I. After all, I was one of His creatures. I was a living being just like all the other living things I saw around me. I came to understand that God would give me the wisdom I needed to succeed in the purpose of my life.

He will supply that wisdom to you, too.

When an individual comes up to me saying, "I have this great opportunity; could you please put together a business plan for me?" I tell that person, "Yes, I could, but I won't. I'm not going to be a part of your failure."

That individual needs to learn the language for himself or herself in order to succeed. Everything in life has a process, and the process of becoming successful in business and industry requires research.

If God has called you to business, He also will show you the pathway to wisdom and understanding regarding that business. Why not sit down and go through some structured courses? Take your time and learn the things you need to know about your product or business idea.

Yeshua went through thirty years of structured training before God released Him into ministry. He became, and still is, the greatest CEO who ever lived, and His product—salvation—is still the most powerful kingdom business concept on Earth today.

WRITE THE VISION

The Bible tells us, "Write the vision, and make it plain upon tables, that he my run that readeth it" (Hab. 2:2, KJV).

What all of us need to understand about success and wealth is that it's a mentality. Our NxLevel™ Entreprenuer Training Institute and business seminars teach what is takes to go through every phase of starting your own business and becoming successful in it. We impart the principles that took me years to discover and learn. But the first, most basic step is "knowing" the vision and recording it. To be successful in your business you must write out a business plan.

God gave me the visions for the businesses I started over the years. Today, I've successfully launched many businesses and have helped others successfully launch their visions for business. Still, a lot of people come up to me and say, "Man, God gave me this idea." They begin discussing their ideas with me, and I listen patiently. Then I ask one defining question, and based upon their answer to this question I know immediately whether or not they will succeed or fail. When I ask this question I often get total silence as the only response.

I ask, "Let me see your vision for business in writing?"

When you go into a business situation with any investor, or when you come into my office to speak with me about your business, this is what you'll hear: "Just let me see what you've got."

The first thing anyone will ask you for is your business plan. You need to be able to show where you're going and how you plan to get there. If you haven't written down your vision, and you haven't made it plain so that others can take it and run with it, then you're not ready to start your business. It's that simple.

The second thing that I hear very often in my seminars is: "All I need to make this vision happen is money."

Although you may be completely convinced that this is so, it's simply not true. For if the God we serve gives us a vision, He will also provide the resources to launch that vision.

MAXIMIZING THE POWER OF UNDERSTANDING

As a young man, I intuitively came to understand that I needed to gain wisdom and understanding to become successful in my life. I needed God to impart that understanding to me just as He had freely given it to the animals in the fields that surrounded me.

So desperate was I to understand the purposes of my life that I even sat down and had a heart-to-heart with a wolf. Through that miraculous experience, I believe that God was giving me a sign to let me know that He was listening to me. He heard me and was answering my questions. In time, He would provide me with the wisdom I needed for success.

Years later, I look back on those lonely experiences and smile. I can see God's sovereign, fatherly hand in my life and how it was that He granted me the understanding I so desperately needed. I'm sharing these experiences with you so that you, too, can come to understand that God is hearing the cry of your soul for success. He will grant you the wisdom and understanding you need to succeed at your purpose in life—just as He did with me.

CHAPTER 4

MAXIMIZING THE POWER OF PERFORMANCE

When I was about fourteen years old, I told my grandmother that I wanted to help out. I took over cutting and hauling the firewood and the coal. I bought a chainsaw from some friends and used it to cut firewood, so that we never again had to buy wood. Every morning I got up extra early and made a fire to warm the house. So I became a man and took over these responsibilities from my grandmother.

I told her, "Grandma, just stay in bed until I get the fire going in the wintertime, and then everybody can get up." That was a wonderful luxury to her, and I felt proud about assuming more responsibility.

I chopped cotton every summer to help make ends meet. When I came back from the fields each week with my pay, I gave her all the money. I never kept back anything. She would resist, saying, "Well, keep a couple of dollars so you can get your lunch."

"Grandma, I don't want anything."

When my sisters and brothers asked her for money she got them everything. She'd go shopping with my money to get them school clothes. I said, "Grandma, I don't want anything. I want you to have something." I would buy things for her and she would take them back, saying, "Son, God is going to take care of Grandma. My responsibility is to raise you."

As I mentioned earlier, my determination and hard work at basketball paid off and I was given a scholarship to attend college as a basketball player. I attended Mississippi County Community College in my first year, and transferred to Arkansas State for my second year.

One evening after a game, the guys invited me out and I drank a few beers. I went back to my dorm and promised myself that I would never drink again. However, drinking became a habit, and eventually I began smoking marijuana as well. These habits led to me hanging around people who smoked marijuana and drank as a lifestyle.

Eventually, my basketball game began to suffer. I was getting ready to learn a valuable lesson about what happens to you when you turn away from God and start walking in sin.

I came to Arkansas State a disciplined youth, but as a star basketball player I got lots of opportunities to date. It wasn't long before I was introduced to sex, which was totally against the values Grandma had taught me. I was becoming increasingly fond of these habits even though I always maintained a sense of control. That second year in Arkansas State I fell while playing ball and injured my knee, and it affected my jumping ability. I got mad at the coach, and that was the end of my basketball career. It took me years to realize that sin had consequences. I had opened up my life to sin and my basketball career died—thus helping me understand that the wages of sin is death.

MEETING ANOTHER UNCLE—UNCLE SAM

I got so mad at my coach that I said, "Forget it! I'm going to join the Air Force. They have a great basketball program in the military. The recruiter told me all about it. You get to travel and play sports all over the country."

Well, guess what? They tell you those things to get you to join. One of my friends and I decided to enlist on the buddy plan. But when the time came to actually go he never showed up. So there I was all by myself.

I told myself that I would finally be able to keep my promises to my grandmother. The military had promised me a good education, training, and a good salary. After I left my grandmother's house and went out on my own, my life had spun out of control. Although I worked hard when I lived with my grandmother, outside influences and a lack of discipline took over when I lived on my own. So I decided that the military was also going to teach me the discipline I lacked.

But when my buddy didn't show up as I was getting on that bus, I kept telling the driver, "Wait! Wait! Wait! Willie, my friend, is coming, and you can't leave until he gets here, because we're on the buddy plan."

The driver was reassuring. He said, "He's probably on another bus. Don't worry about it, because they'll pick him up."

I said, "Okay," and I didn't worry. But he never came; he chickened out. The only reason I went through with enlisting was because we had planned to do it together. I never would have gone through with it alone. Getting on that bus all by myself was one of the scariest moments of my life.

That bus drove us all the way to San Antonio, Texas, where an officer boarded and starting yelling. "From now on, I'm your mother and your father."

Oh, my God, I thought, panicking inside. I leaned over towards the bus driver and said, "Listen, I want to stay on the bus. You've got to take me back home because I came on the buddy plan, and I'm not supposed to be here."

Kindly, he responded, "Okay, just stand right here by the bus and be the last one in the back of the line. When I get ready to pull off I'll call you, and you can just get back on."

"Okay, okay. Thank you so much, because I know this is a mistake. I'll just leave my bag here."

With that he closed that bus door and pulled away with my bag. So there I was in the rain, terrified, having never been out of the sticks of Arkansas except to visit my uncle in Michigan.

I didn't hear the drill instructor when he yelled, "When I call your name I want you to repeat your whole name. Say 'Sir, here.'" I hadn't heard what he said, so when he called, "Jerome Edmondson," I said, "Right here."

He looked up with rage in his eyes and said, "Jerome Edmonson."

I said, "Right here."

This guy made his way through the line of people military-style and ended up right in my face. He laid his fingertip on my forehead and said, "They probably told you that in the military we couldn't hit you, didn't they?"

I said, "Yes, sir."

And he knocked me on the ground. Then he stood me up and said, "When I call your name, you repeat your name and say 'Sir, here.'"

I was crying, *Oh, my God*. When he called my name I said, "Jerome Edmonson. Sir, here." I was trying not to let him know I was crying. I wanted him to think that rain was falling in my face.

After they gave us military-issue clothing, I went into the bathroom and prayed hard. *Oh, my God. God, please help me; please help me. I'm sorry for all my sin. If you help me to get through all of this, I'll stop sinning and I'll live my life for You from now on.* I made a promise to God to live for Him, and I intended to keep it this time.

The next day they assigned me as dorm chief, and I was put in charge of the entire dorm. So I started playing basketball in the military, and I attended community college at the Air Force. But what the military really did for me was to bring discipline into my life. Before long, I adjusted to military life quite well and started to enjoy it.

BREAKING MY PROMISE

It wasn't long before I began to break my promise to God. I began partying, hanging out, and having fun. Once again, I was destroying the values and lessons I learned in those fields of dreams. At the time I thought I was really living it up, but in truth I was slowly dying; I just didn't realize it yet.

I did a couple of overseas tours of duty, then ended up at Little Rock Air Force Base in Arkansas in my fourth year in the military. And that's where my military career ended. I was sharing a dorm with a guy who sold drugs.

He didn't stay in the barracks; he lived off base with his girlfriend. So I had a room to myself, a prized situation in the military.

I continued to pray no matter how drunk I got. Grandma had said, "Pray every night before you go to bed." So I was praying drunk, hung over, and torn apart. I didn't do drugs in the military, but I sure did drink a lot on weekends. I would stumble into bed drunk at night, get on my knees and say, "Father, I just want to come to you before I go to sleep." Then I would roll over and go to sleep.

Grandma had told me not to lay my head down in sleep, no matter what condition I was in, without praying to God first.

That year the Feds went after my roommate for selling drugs. One day, when I went to perform my duty guarding a top-secret missile complex, I found the law enforcement people waiting at the gate for me. They said, "Airman First Class Edmonson, release your weapon."

I said, "I cannot give my weapon to anyone."

And they said, "Well, we've been ordered to take your weapon from you and seize this military vehicle."

I said, "It can't happen, I'm sorry. You need to have my commanding officer report to me."

So my commanding officer came down there and said, "Sergeant Edmonson, we have to relieve you of your weapon."

They told me, "We've arrested your partner, and we know that you guys are running a very heavy drug operation here at Little Rock Air Force Base, supplying drugs to surrounding neighborhoods and to folks in the military. He's already given us your name."

I said, "What are you talking about?"

"You and your roommate are going to prison," they said.

My drill instructor snatched my stripes off my uniform and placed me on limited duty. I realized that once that happened it was the death of me. My military career was over.

I prayed, *God, how could this happen to me? I've done nothing...I'm innocent of this.*

Although I truly was innocent of the charges and fought very hard to clear my name, the false accusation hanging over my head was enough to destroy my future in the military. My battle to clear my name ended up in the press, which started to make the military look very bad. Eventually, my military attorney convinced me that my best course of action was to take an honorable discharge. He said, "We'll give you an honorable discharge, and we'll get you out of the military and let you go on with your life. There's no longer a career here for you, Jerome." I had to accept the harsh reality that my career in the military would forever be marred by the charges—albeit false—that had been levied against me.

PERFORMANCE IS MEASURED BY THE SPEED OF RECOVERY

I had to leave the military. After I packed up all my belongings, I sat there and cried. *God, why me? Why did this thing happen to me when I'm innocent?*

My Uncle Bill invited me to come to Pontiac, Michigan, and live with him. He said, "Son, why don't you just come up here? Don't go back down South, because there's nothing there for you."

As I sat on the plane flying to Michigan, feeling as if I had lost everything, I remembered my vow to God. I had promised Him that if He helped me that I would live differently. He kept His part, but I had broken my promise to Him again and had returned to sin. I had failed the test.

Nevertheless, God had protected me. My roommate had gone to prison, and I could have ended up there with him on false charges. Going to Michigan was my destiny. Although I didn't know it at the time, it was there that I would meet my wife and enter the business world.

Furthermore, the time I spent in the military had not gone to waste. It had imparted discipline that I desperately needed. I learned how to take the work ethic I grew up with and implement it in my own life. Ever since then, hard work has been a key factor to my many successes in life.

Joining the Workforce

Once, in Pontiac, Michigan, my uncle asked, "Jerome, why don't you just get a job here?"

I said, "No, you know I've got to go back down South and take care of Grandma. Uncle Bill, you know how it is; she has no one there."

"Jerome, get a job here so that you can make a difference. There's nothing for you back there; if you really want to help her, help yourself first."

He was right, and I knew it. I could do little to help my grandmother by going back to the dusty gravel roads of Arkansas and Missouri. There were no opportunities for me there, and I would eventually end up falling prey to the low expectations that went along with that lifestyle. I chose to do better.

I landed a job with a collection agency making good money. I bought a car, and life started to take on new meaning for me. I felt as though I had finally escaped from the Egypt of my past.

THE SPIRIT OF APPLICATION

One of the keys to success in everything I've ever done is the development of a "spirit of application." That simply means developing the ability to take the things you learn and apply them to your life.

I learned how to work by watching my grandmother work tirelessly, day in and day out. But it wasn't until I began to apply the many lessons about work that she taught me through her example that my own life changed for the better.

She also taught me not to drink, do drugs, and become sexually active before marriage. God taught me a great deal as a Heavenly Father as I roamed those fields and prayed in my own way. But after I left home I became a hearer but not a doer. I knew the right thing to do, but I wasn't applying those principles to the life I was pursuing.

The spirit of application is the key to performance. When you begin taking the kingdom principles you've learned and applying them to every aspect of your life, success will follow without effort. People can model things for you, and they can tell you all you need to know. But until you take godly principles and make them your own, they will continue to be useless to you. Your ability to apply knowledge is key to everything you do in life.

Paraphrased, James 1:22-25 tells us not to merely listen to the Word and so deceive ourselves. We must do what it says. And anyone who listens to the Word but does not do what it says is like a man who looks at his face in the mirror, and after looking at himself, goes away, and immediately forgets what he looks like. But the man who looks intently into the perfect law that gives freedom, and continues to do this, not forgetting what he has heard, but doing it, will be blessed in what he does.

The Bible says that doers are blessed, not hearers. Today I teach a sixteen-week entrepreneurial training course, and in nearly every class someone drops out in the middle. Once, I went up to a particular pastor and asked him why he had dropped out. I was devastated at what I heard coming from the mouth of this individual who leads thousands of people. He said, "Well, the Lord showed me what I'm supposed to do. I thank you for just spending time with me." That man didn't do any work, and he didn't turn in one piece of homework. He said, "The Lord showed me."

I sat in front of him asking questions. "What is your goal? How are you going to reach it? What is your plan?"

"Well, God is going to make a way somehow; I'm just trusting in the Lord."

Do you know what? In less than a month that individual lost his church. The business plan that he had intended to create would have taken his church out of the financial situation it was in. He received the information he needed, but he did not apply that information through work.

SUCCESS WITHOUT WORK

Too many of us desire success without work. However, success and work are one concept. It's not possible to succeed without working diligently.

The Word of God says that God took the Israelites into the wilderness for this reason: to release their minds from the slave mentality and prepare them for the Promised Land by giving them the power to get wealth. Deuteronomy 8:18 says, "Thou shalt remember [what I have taught you through this wilderness experience] the Lord thy God: for it is He that giveth thee power to get wealth" (KJV).

God gave them this power, and He has given that power to you, too. It was a promise from the beginning. Therefore, wealth is your inheritance; it's the promise. So why are you begging for something that you already have? Why are you pleading with and trying to manipulate God for what He's already given you the ability to receive? Your promises are but a relationship away from overflowing in your life.

FAITH WITHOUT WORKS

The question you need to be asking yourself is: How much do you want wealth? Wanting won't bring wealth to you, but working will. Now, this is the arena in which we fail most often, and I'll tell you why. Because faith is a verb—it requires action and not merely belief. That is why without work faith is just a word you use in an attempt to manipulate God. Very simply, it's dead.

As the body without the spirit is dead, so faith without works is dead. If a man or woman doesn't work, guess what? That person won't eat.

Let me share something with you that I want you to clearly understand. There is no excuse for poverty, and there is no excuse for not having anything. God has given you the power to get wealth, and learning to work is part of that power. You can go out there and put your mind to anything and succeed at it if you work hard.

Grandma raised me well, and my work ethic is the best. If you're a kingdom citizen, then you've disqualified yourself according to the world's standards. Obedience to God in your life will reap a great reward and harvest for others. If you haven't found something worth living for, other than yourself, you have failed God and thus are reaping the benefits of your lack of labor. Until I became obedient to the commands of God, it didn't matter how much I knew or how hard I tried; everything was temporary. When I became a doer of the things I knew to do, I became a continual success, because I was starting to become the person God created me to be.

You can rebel against God, as I did, and find what the world has in store for you. But its only interest in you is to steal, kill, and destroy you. However, if you decide to succeed, then success is yours, and the power to achieve that success is a seed that has been in you from the day God birthed you on planet earth. However, without a vision, a purpose, and a destiny for your existence God cannot and will not release abundance in your life.

Not knowing your purpose in life means that you have made a decision to merely exist. One day when He comes you will then fly, fly away—oh glory! Do you really think that God has secured a place for you in glory after you have done nothing for His kingdom here on Earth? I tell my students to work as if everything depends on you and pray as if everything depends on God!

HOLDING ONTO SUCCESS

Developing your work ethic is essential for succeeding, but once you've achieved success you'll find that holding onto success will take just as much or more work. You'll never arrive, for the ability to sustain success and follow the principles of God while prospering is a serious challenge in a sinful world.

It takes time and energy to succeed and to maintain success. You'll never get to the place where you can sit back and say, *Hallelujah, I made it.* That's why your work ethic must become as much a part of you as the way you talk and the way you walk.

Your burden of responsibility only increases as you become more successful. At times you will feel that you're in an upside-down triangle with the world on your shoulders. Everyone seems to be depending on you to help direct their lives, and if you fail, all those lives will come tumbling down. That's the burden of responsibility we must bear.

The Word of God encourages you to let your light so shine before men that they can see your good works. People are watching you, and when you've become successful you'll also find that people need you. They depend upon you, and it's important not to let them down. While you're on the road of kingdom success, ethics and integrity are paramount.

Chapter 5

Maximizing the Gift of Success

Working at the collection agency was a good beginning, but I really wasn't making much money. I got a second job selling vacuum cleaners called Filter Queens. I spent my days going door to door cleaning filthy carpets for free in hope of making a $200 commission on a sale. Therefore you can imagine how intrigued I was when a headhunter called me with some new employment possibilities.

He asked me how interested I'd be in a career in the food industry.

"Where?" I asked.

"Kentucky Fried Chicken," he said.

"No way!"

He went on to explain that it was a management position, which paid $25,000 to $28,000 a year—a lot more than I was earning at the collection agency and on my knees selling Filter Queens.

So I said, "I'll go for that."

I completed a test and entered KFC's fast-track program. As I began to work in the business world, I started to feel as if I'd found my niche. I was discovering myself in a whole new way. KFC, this new piece of self-discovery, seemed to be creating an entire picture of who I was meant to be. I was touching my own destiny and purpose, and that felt very satisfying.

Working in a restaurant, which I had once dreaded, was exciting and stimulating. I was being given the opportunity to be in charge of people, make decisions, and help people. I thought, *This is it. I love this...this is what I want to do.*

I shot through the fast-track training program, finishing early. It was a six-month program, and I completed it in four. I came out already operating as a restaurant manager in a store, and after a year I was a training manager with my own store. I felt like a fish in water.

Before long, KFC put me in a second store, and within two years I was an area manager with eight stores under my supervision. That led to my becoming an area manager with thirteen stores. My entire tenure with KFC lasted from 1987 to 1993. During that time, I became one of the most celebrated young stars ever to enter the KFC system. I was the youngest individual ever to hold the President's Award and for two years had the highest volume sales and profits in the company.

In 1992, my stores led the entire nation in sales and profits. I developed more managers and more assistant managers for KFC than anyone had before in any market. I became known as a management development guru. I oversaw shift supervisors and managers in all my stores and was able run my restaurants using the telephone and a laptop to communicate to my high-performance leaders.

I had entered into this entirely new world of business with very little preparation. In truth, I went from the cotton fields of Arkansas to the business world in very short order. It seemed that in one breath I was chopping cotton in a place where I had very little hope of achievement, and in the next I was running several multimillion-dollar restaurants.

PASSION FOR PEOPLE

All of my stores were located in the inner city of Detroit, and what drove my passion for success as a leader of those urban KFC stores was the people. Those inner-city stores saw some of the highest-volume sales in the entire franchise, yet the people who worked there were highly undervalued. My quest became to inspire them to see and become who they really were: not just workforce employees, but people of purpose.

District managers rarely visited the city stores. They felt threatened coming into those areas, even though they netted some of the greatest sales. The corporation's new furnishings, fresh equipment, crisp décor, and strong monetary incentives usually were invested everywhere. But the city stores were forced to use wire clothes hangers to hold cooking cabinets together. The young, talented, hardworking employees in the urban stores wore uniforms that were greasy, torn, and ragged, and worked in kitchens that were infested with roaches and rats. If customers had known what was going on in the back, they might never have bought chicken out front.

We would open up a bag of flour and have to sift the roaches out of it. We had a saying that we repeated again and again: there was almost nothing that 360 degrees couldn't kill once you put it in the fryer. Nevertheless, the filthy conditions were disgusting.

THE AFRICAN-AMERICAN MENU

I brought a fresh vision into those KFC establishments. I started using the money they wanted us to add to the bottom line to take some risks. I called it thinking outside the box, and I began developing those stores and investing in the people who made the company a success.

One of my brainchildren was called the "African-American Menu," and it enjoyed enormous success. This was my first breakthrough as the new leader I had so suddenly become in the world of business.

The African-American Menu was used in more than five hundred restaurants nationwide, and that year my bonus checks for the innovation exceeded my paycheck by three times. This menu idea was the key to our leading the nation in sales and profits that year. I received many other accolades, which helped to boost my confidence as a business leader.

Yet the African-American Menu seemed all too obvious. It entailed little more than changing the side dishes to ones that people liked. Many of the traditional foods in the African-American community come from the South, and Southern folk don't serve macaroni salad and potato salad with fried chicken. They enjoy side dishes like macaroni and cheese, greens, cornbread, and sweet potato pie. We put these on the African-American Menu, and achieved great success.

The menu innovation simply involved tailoring our offerings to meet the demands of the urban marketplace. In other words, I knew my industry and my customer. By implementing few changes our bottom line started to soar.

MAXIMIZING MOTIVATION

What happened in Detroit held the potential to impact nationwide sales. Therefore, Detroit became a test market for the rest of the country. It wasn't long before the African-American Menu blitzed the rest of the nation.

At the same time, a fire was ignited inside of me. I was realizing that my gifts were powerful and could make a difference. The impact of that reality started to burn inside of me, and that internal combustion would fuel a fire of motivation that would drive me further and further towards my goals.

I had started to maximize my misfortune in a fundamental way. I was taking the simple things that I had been given—gifts, abilities, and tastes—and turning them into keys for success.

I continued to have a burning desire within me to be something more than people had told me I would become. I wanted to make my grandma proud of me, and to show my uncle that he made the right choice in taking a chance on me. Achieving success was a way of thanking my uncle for bringing me to the city and giving me an opportunity.

A PASSION TO SUCCEED

The passion for success I experienced was not for myself. Glorifying Jerome never even crossed my mind. I wanted to be something for others. I wanted others to see my good works, and I wanted them to see who I was. I gave God all the glory. Everybody who knew me knew that I loved God and always spoke of Him. My deepest passion was a passion for God. My employees were convicted and converted because they saw my performance and my work ethic, and they knew that it stemmed from my passion for God.

85

I was letting my light so shine before men that they might see my good works and glorify my heavenly Father. People said, "Well, if this is how God cleans you up, if this is the leadership He places in you, and if this is what you can get by serving God, than I want to serve Him. Jerome, I want to go to church with you."

From the cooks to the janitors, my employees would go to church with me on Sundays. For my part, I was becoming increasingly excited about the business world—the possibilities seemed limitless.

RIDING HIGH

I was at the height of my career in the business world. I was sponsoring scholarship programs in the city of Detroit. The vice president, the chairman, and the CEO of KFC would call me direct. Detroit's mayor, Coleman Young, one of the best mayors the city ever had, respected me and saw me as a great community example. I was earning a reputation with great acclaim. The mayor even hosted a benefit on my behalf with KFC's president in attendance in one of the classiest spots in town, the Renaissance Ballroom.

While working with the marketing department, I decided that we should do our own commercials. They became enormous motivators and morale boosters. We put our best employees on the radio. Their voices would come over the air: "Hi! This is Joyce at restaurant number 122 on Chalmers. Let me tell you about our new KFC special this month."

That young person would go home and announce, "Mamma, listen—I'm on the radio." It was another idea that really started to pump up our market. People were saying, "Jerome puts his people on the radio. He's a real asset to his community."

Several of our stores were being robbed quite often. My response was to hire some homeless vagrants who hung around the store all the time. I handed them brooms and dustpans and said, "Now, this is your job. Every morning and throughout the day, three times a day, I want you to make sure that the parking lot is clean. In addition, make sure no thieves hang around the store. For this you will receive two hot meals a day, and at the end of the week I'll give you a little money."

Do you know what happened? The break-ins stopped. When someone did try to break in, these guys knew exactly who it was, and they could take the police right to his house. They knew the community better than anybody because they saw everything that happened in the dark.

The other vagrants couldn't hang around the store anymore because of the territorial codes that existed between these street people. KFC became off-limits to crime and other elements of street life. The stores became the domain of a particular individual and the others respected it.

THE BEST FROM THE WORST

Maximizing is nothing more than learning to take what you have, the little you've been given—whether it be your gifts, abilities, talents, opportunities, skills, life events, or even the negative things in your life—and making those things work for you in a much greater capacity.

The more I succeeded, the more certain individuals within KFC started to work against me in an attempt to set me up to fail. When I became an area manager, they realigned the areas and gave me the worst stores. I guess they thought I would have to fail, but they didn't realize that I came from an even worse environment. I enjoyed the challenge of turning such stores around and making them profitable, clean, safe, and an asset to the company and the communities in which we did business.

So I made the best out of the worst, which is part of what maximizing is all about. I understood the conditions that these people had to endure. I understood that these folks had no work ethic and no values because they felt that nobody cared. The employees at these stores felt the impact of the negative corporate attitudes towards them. They believed that KFC was pulling money out of the community, but didn't care at all about the patrons, the neighborhoods, the employees and their conditions, or the stores.

When I was handed these stores I became determined to change the company mind-set. I felt that it didn't matter what the corporate people thought or didn't think, understood or didn't understand. What mattered was who and what those employees were going to become. I became determined to affect the destiny of the individuals placed under my charge.

You can't live your life feeling like the victim of someone else's failure, faults, shortcomings, and sins. You've got to become somebody, no matter what others have handed to you. Therefore, I began to conduct coaching sessions with my managers and employees. It was my ongoing relationship to Jesus Christ that gave me the capacity to genuinely care about these young people, and to have the ability to effect a change within them.

One of the first things I did was to purchase new uniforms for all of the employees. I made them throw away those dirty, tattered uniforms, and I ordered three sets of new ones for each one of them.

I said, "Now, how do you guys feel? Because if you feel good coming to work then you're going to perform according to the way you feel." I even went out and purchased ironing boards and irons for the backs of the stores. If people came in with wrinkled uniforms, I made them iron them before they started their shifts. My employees all looked sharp.

At the end of the day, I would close down the stores and clean those kitchens, bathrooms, and eating areas until they shined. We had the entire crew in to hose down the walls and clean every crack and corner. Then we'd throw out the garbage. The very next morning, I would have pest control companies come through and rid those facilities of insects and rats.

It was my relationship with Yeshua that gave me the wisdom I needed to succeed, no matter what obstacles were thrown my way. It was also God's wisdom to love and develop the people under my charge. Yeshua loved people, and it didn't matter to Him if someone was rich or a prostitute or a thief; God is no respecter of persons. I was learning to maximize the power of performance in my team, which I will discuss in more detail later on in this book. My relationship with God was the key to my success. He breathed compassion into me even for the vagrants out there on the street, to the point that I didn't kick them out of my stores for hanging around, but developed ways to empower them and help them help me.

Those homeless men and women became my non-salaried employees, and I put twenty bucks into their pockets at the end of the week and gave them two hot meals a day. You know what? When I was inspected, I was never marked off for not having clean parking lots. Those homeless leaders even pulled the weeds around the bushes, and they were always respectful to the customers.

The word kept going out about what was happening, and before long newspaper reporters were calling and asking to interview me about the innovative changes taking place at KFC. All that only brought even more attention and traffic into our stores. The *Detroit Free Press* wrote several glowing pieces about our success and the our community involvement.

We started handing out scholarships to hardworking young people in the various neighborhoods, and increasingly I was becoming a role model in the community. I was at the peak of my career riding a wave of success, and it felt great.

The Pitfalls, Snares, and Traps of Success

My desire for success was all about my drive to be the best. I had taken a hoe and chopped weeds and vines around cotton with the same passion and striving for excellence that I used while cooking chicken and sweeping parking lots at KFC.

Nevertheless, it seemed that it was all happening very quickly, and I didn't have the time to learn from the hard knocks that can accompany success in an individual's life. I was so busy enjoying my victory that I became blinded to the darker side of success, the weeds that can grow up inside a human soul when he or she is looking the other way. Little did I realize that my good fortune would change and that my time of success would be short-lived.

As I achieved one accomplishment after another, I started to become addicted to pride. I was riding high, but I started to forget about God and was headed for a major fall.

Success came to me suddenly, and I was ill-prepared to handle the pitfalls of pride that often accompany success.

The disease of pride started to poison my soul, just a little at first, but very quickly I became completed tainted by it. I was hanging out with the "who's who" in the business world, and once again I forgot about the promises that I had made to God.

Suddenly, I had become an arrogant, successful guy in the business world. The devil is cunning and will wait for the opportune time to show back up in your life and tempt you with the desires you thought were gone. Let's get one this straight before I move forward with what's about to happen in my life. The devil has no power to make you do anything. Every day that you wake up on God's great earth you have a choice of life and death. His Word says, "Choose this day whom ye will serve" (Josh. 24:15, KJV), and every day we make our decisions to choose life or death. Sin is always all about making choices.

My attitudes began to change, ever so subtly. My vocabulary went from *glory to God* to *glory to me*. Pride was rooting itself into my spirit, and its effect would prove disastrous.

I talked about God a lot, but spoke His blessings less and less. I started to pride myself on my own abilities. Suddenly, I was the one who had made it. Before long, I was back in the nightclubs partying again. Armed with an expense account, I was now the man around town. I was living my dream all right, but I was forgetting the pathway I had taken to get there.

Like the disease of cancer, pride was growing in my soul and afflicting it with a kind of moral sickness.

Man, I don't have to do my paperwork right now, I might tell myself. Or I might simply choose not to show up for work. The integrity that was once as normal a part of my life and work as breathing was becoming increasingly compromised.

All the values that I had in place to get me to where I was were gradually changing. The deception of pride was luring me into an arena in which I was behaving and thinking very differently. I told myself that I had made it, that I was now successful. I had arrived. However, I didn't understand that success is not a level that you reach. It is plateau that you must maintain even more diligently and carefully once you've arrived there.

My newly-discovered fame and fortune also cemented within me a sense of loyalty to the company, and with it came an exaggerated sense of dependence upon the company. Now I was a company man. I was Mr. KFC. As a matter of fact, when folks met me on the street they called me Mr. Chicken. That's where I spent most of my time.

I was a loyal corporate citizen, and I completely expected doors to keep blasting open in front of me. People said, "Jerome, if you continue achieving at this rate, you're going to become a vice president." These were the carrots that were being waved in front of me, the lures that enticed me to chase after promises with increasing vigor.

When it came time for my performance reviews I got very high marks. I was told, "Okay, Jerome, now you need to finish your degree." I had attended community college at Arkansas State and in the Air Force, but had never graduated. Before I could hope to become a vice president, I would need to finish that degree.

So despite my rigorous workload at the stores I went back to school and attended classes to complete my undergraduate degree. I invested even more time in the company. I was becoming what they wanted me to be, and my advances were moving me ever closer to a glass ceiling that I had yet to understand.

I sacrificed everything on that altar of compromise, even my faith. I told myself, *God understands that I have to work on Sundays. My employees have to work on Sundays, and so should I.* I was being lured by my own success in the business world, and I didn't realize that sooner or later it would destroy me.

Who Was This New Jerome?

Now I had the power to tell a person, "You're terminated!" and end his or her career. There's no doubt about it—I became very arrogant. If someone talked back to me, I fired him and ordered him out of my store without waiting to learn about other circumstances that might have been involved. I never worried about the consequences of such actions, either. It didn't matter if that individual had children at home. If he or she was going through something, I still felt that that person should have known better.

Out of nowhere I had developed an *I don't care* attitude. "I'm the boss here. I'm the leader. I make the rules here, and if you don't like what I say then you're terminated." Period. Who was this new Jerome?

I didn't realize it at the time, but my newly-developing arrogance was a sign that I couldn't handle success. I was living in the midst of success with no clue about how to manage all the perks and pleasures—all the things that came with it.

I also felt empowered at church. I got to sit in the front row. I was head of the deacon board and a trustee. I was one of the Sunday school teachers. The pastor mentioned my name from the pulpit when he saw me. "It's good to see Jerome Edmonson at church this morning," he'd say. When it came time to give offerings, if five people went up front to give $100, I would be the first one up. I gave extra money in church so that the pastor would keep recognizing me before the congregation.

I told myself that I was really doing something. I was really helping the church and the community. But I was becoming increasingly rude and demanding. I enjoyed wielding the power of authority. I was forgetting the simple virtues of kindness, giving, generosity, and humility that I had learned and relearned at my grandmother's knee. I was even defining and managing my relationship with Christ, determining what I wanted it to be rather than allowing Him to determine what He wanted it to be. I could write a check instead of praying about what I needed. I was in control.

LOVED AND HATED

My employees went from loving me to hating me. My managers began to call in sick more often. I started having more and more problems at work. One manager called the corporate office and said that I was drinking in the parking lot with my employees, and I was written up for it.

That manager was a marked man after that. Needless to say, he was fired. I felt it was important to make an example of him. I wanted people to know that if they crossed me there would be severe consequences.

Even my boss said, "It's probably best if you get rid of that employee, but do it right." They gave me their approval to fire him, because the corporate culture didn't like tattle-tales.

I had gone from a loving people-developer to a passive negotiator who continually played games of power with the employees to make them perform. I'd say, "You know better than that! The next time you're fired." I learned to become a documenter, writing up employees for the smallest infractions. The corporation seemed to love such behavior.

Sadly, it never dawned on me that I had changed. I told myself that I had a standard to uphold. I was looked up to in the company, and I needed everything to be right. During staff meetings I never missed an opportunity to remind everyone of my successes. I would gloat, "When I came into this market, you guys had nothing. No one in the corporation even cared about you. If you don't do things the way I've taught or, better yet, my way, you'll be fired or you'll be written up"

It was my way or the highway. I had never talked like that in my life, but now I was barking harsh commands to everyone. I went from training, encouraging, and motivating my staff to running a dictatorship. I stopped wearing uniforms or KFC shirts. Instead, I wore suits and ties. When I walked into a store I had on nice clothes. My appearance made it clear that I wasn't mopping floors and wiping down counters anymore. I had arrived at the level of superiority. If I saw something that needed doing, I would professionally demand, "Get the manager in here now. Where's he at?"

I was making enemies left and right, and those enemies would prove to be my undoing. Those managers who didn't give me problems became my favorites, and for the first time a sense of division entered our team.

The corporation came out with a performance review program. In it they gave all my people the opportunity to write down how they felt about me as a manager, and the employees weren't required to identify themselves. When I received those reports I was devastated at how some of my people spoke about me. They really didn't like me at all.

My image in the corporation started to change, too. In addition, there remained a high degree of prejudice at the corporate level, as well as jealousies and political jockeying that I knew little about. In that area in Michigan, it was extremely uncommon for a black person to be in such a prominent position. I didn't have to answer to the regional managers. I had direct connections at the highest corporate levels, which only made the regional managers angry. I could get on the phone and call the president of human resources when I disagreed with something at the regional level. I did this quite often because of my arrogance. When people made me angry or picked on me, which happened regularly, then I would go over their heads to corporate. I even got my director of operations fired, which only increased the building resentment against me.

The individual who replaced the fired director had it in for me, and she started conducting private meetings with my managers and employees in order to gather ammunition against me.

Termination

Nevertheless, I rested in a false security that this company would take care of me. I was in a high position, and I felt very secure—totally invincible. I no longer placed my security in my relationship with God, which had gotten me to where I was.

Other factors came into play as well. I decided that I wanted to become a franchisee, and so I began to talk to the vice president of franchise operations. The vice president of corporate operations wanted me to grow within the company and demanded that I quit talking to the franchise person. And the franchise person said, "Well, you can't do that, because we want to make franchisees too, and the area managers make good franchisees." So now I was in the middle of a war between these two corporate factions.

In addition, a decision had been made to get rid of me, of which I was completely unaware. My performance appraisals changed. Moreover, the new director of operations demanded that I tell her where I was at every hour of the day.

In the midst of all of this stress, I suffered an angina attack, and the doctor put me on a six-month leave of absence. During that hiatus, right before Thanksgiving of that year, I got a call from the corporate office. I was told, "Mr. Edmonson, I just wanted to call and let you know that you're not going to get a check. Corporate has stopped your payroll."

Afterward, on February 14, 1993, I received a letter terminating my employment.

WHAT GOES AROUND

I had felt secure in corporate America; being fired was the last thing I expected. But there's no doubt in my mind that what goes around comes around. You've got to be careful how you treat people, because you never know when these things will come back around to you.

My job was gone, and with it went everything I had worked for. My career, all those people whom I cared about and loved, all the things I had achieved, all the people I put in position, the folks who knew me in the community, the pride, the relationships, the mayors, my sense of security—it was all gone. I was devastated.

I had built myself up in my own mind to the point at which I considered myself invincible. I, I, I—it was all about me, and I could not even save myself. I thought my own work ethic would keep me up there no matter what happened. I placed myself on a pedestal and it collapsed beneath me. I was left feeling like a hopeless loser, too embarrassed to face people and tell them what happened. I simply started lying, and a spirit of lying took over my life because I didn't want my peers to know I had been terminated.

The Bible says that pride comes before destruction and a haughty spirit before a fall, and when that fall comes it brings with it a hurt that is beyond belief. For a while I attempted to keep up a façade of employment, spending all my savings, telling people that I was involved in consulting work and never missing the opportunity to drop the names of prominent people I knew. But inside I was completely crushed.

At my lowest point, I remember riding in my truck down Eight-Mile Road, crying, with a .357 Magnum in my hand, telling myself, *I'm going to end it right now.* I was getting ready to end it all. I had accelerated to a high speed, and I figured that I'd shoot myself and the truck would go off the road and just crash into something. But I couldn't go through with it; I just couldn't take my life. I pulled over at a gas station and tears streamed down my face. I had let everyone down, but somehow I knew that ending my life was not the answer. So I dried my face and went home and survived another lonely night.

CHAPTER 6

MAXIMIZING FAILURE AND THE POWER OF FAITH

I was unemployed for a year and a half, and that long, painful time emptied my spirit of a lot of the false perceptions I had gained over the previous ten years of work. I had a lot to time to think and unlearn the poisonous understandings I had gained in the workplace. This process of renewing my thinking took my life from unemployment to deployment. After the pain came positioning and power.

MY FRIEND JACK

The first year of unemployment was extremely challenging. So I introduced myself to a lot of new friends. One who became very close to me was named Jack. His last name was Daniels. For nondrinkers, Jack Daniels is a brand of very potent Tennessee whiskey.

When you're miserable and you come home drunk and hung over, you get even more miserable. I was angry and frustrated at the world. One night I came in and sat down on my basement steps in the dark feeling exceptionally sorry for myself. I put my head down in my hand and asked a question that has forever changed my life.

I said, "God, why me?"

I had always been a little leery of people who told me they had heard God's voice. I had been to church all my life and had never heard His voice, or at least identified it as His voice. However, that night He spoke to me, answering my question. He said simply, "Why not?"

I thought someone else was sitting in that dark room. I got up and began checking around the room for whomever had spoken to me, as the voice seemed real and close. I waited another minute and sat back down. I reassured myself, *It must have been that Jack Daniels talking to me.*

Then in the quiet darkness I heard it once more. "Why not you, Jerome? I can use you. If you'll let Me, I can take the termination you've gone through and convert it into determination. I can use this to make you into everything I've called you to be."

I was stunned. God was interested in a loser like me? I had turned my back on Him in the midst of a blessing and He still believed in me?

If you are a business leader, know that there is nothing under the sun that you can do to make God hate you. It's impossible for Him to hate His image. He hates your sin, but He is determined to do anything for His children if they will only obey.

After that evening, I became determined to seek God. I wanted to know who He was, and how living with Him could work for me. I had worked sixty to seventy hours per week for the world, and look how it ended. I would put the same degree of work and determination into knowing God and learning His Word. I decided that I wanted every one of the sixty-six books of the Bible to become a part of my life. The world of business had failed me, so now I wanted to try the world of God. I had nothing to lose.

THE SPEED OF RECOVERY

After that night, I prayed, *God, if you give me another chance, I promise You that I'll never ever turn my back on You again. I'll live my life for You forever. I'm sorry for my ignorance, and I apologize for letting You down.*

I lay down on the couch and fell asleep, and when I woke up I knew I was a new person. I declared that I was ready to change and become somebody completely new. I was ready to take back what was mine—what the enemy of my soul had stolen from me. I would not be defeated by man or by the devil, not even by my own weak flesh.

I realized that I was either going to be totally defeated or I was going to turn it all around and win. God was using the experience of grief and loss to change me deeply, to renew my mind and spirit in order to transform my life. From the pain and ashes of that loss was emerging the power to maximize defeat and failure. God was giving me the ability to go from unemployment to empowerment, from unemployment to deployment. God was working a new thing in me, and everything in my life was getting ready to change.

At the time, I had been unemployed for an entire year. Little did I know that it would be another six months before I was ready to step into my destiny. But God had a plan for me, and He was working all things together for my good. Some years later, I would look back and realize that. But at that time, I could only thank God for sparing my life and breathing hope into my beleaguered, weary soul.

It's important for you to understand that no matter what circumstance you're in, God has a plan to bring you to your destiny if you will only allow Him to do it. Even when my best friend was Jack Daniels, God was still working His plan in my life.

SEIZING PERSONAL EMPOWERMENT

I had been sending out reams of resumes with no response. Nothing was happening, no matter what I did. Nobody was calling me, and nobody was hiring me. I felt as if God had flipped a switch, and where my efforts had once been able to yield a great effect, they had now become impotent. I couldn't make anything happen, no matter how much I tried. It was an extremely frustrating time, and my sense of powerlessness began to wash over me, together with an increasing feeling of emptiness and loss. I was struggling internally and externally.

God had something better in mind for me, although I didn't realize it at first. He was re-creating me, remolding me into what I am now. I needed to go through this kind of experience in order to break my pride and rebellion and cause me to rely upon Him. I had for years developed all these false images and expectations, and I expected God to cleanse me over night.

DESTROYING THE HAUGHTY SPIRIT

God was breaking me, and he was tearing from the thing that I had become in the blindness of my pride. He was ripping apart the things that had become part of me without His approval. He was destroying the spirit of pride that had risen up within my mind and spirit.

God was in control the entire time, although it certainly didn't feel like it. Once He broke me down, He was planning to build me back up. But I didn't really understand all of this then. I really only understood the trauma of it all, for it was a very traumatic time in my life.

From Unemployed to Deployed—Maximizing Priorities

During this time, I had to face the truth about my priorities. God really had not been the first priority of my life. My faith consisted of a lot of lip service, but very little heart service. I sounded like a man of faith in church, but I was living my life in service to myself.

That year and a half of unemployment gave me plenty of time to look at myself in the mirror every morning, and frankly, I didn't much like what I saw. I was selfish. I was using God. In other words, I had defined Him and categorized Him for myself, for what I wanted Him to be, not for what He wanted me to be, nor for who He was.

Along with all of my daily reports and outgoing mail, I had also placed God into a box. Although I never spoke it or even understood it was how I felt, my lifestyle was telling God, *Here's who I think You are, and I'm not going to let You outside the box. I want you to be this for me.*

I was this person who went to church to see on Sunday, and sometimes Wednesday service. When I got into trouble I would ask for forgiveness. God had no place in business as I made thousands of daily decisions. I didn't need Him for that. Therefore, I wasn't maximizing my relationship with Him.

MAXIMIZING THE POWER OF FAITH

However, during that year and a half of unemployment I came to see God very differently. I began to see Him as the total and complete key to all my future success. I took Him out of the box and gave Him first place in my heart, mind, and life.

I found out that God was everything, and He could do exceedingly, abundantly above all I could ask or think. He could lay the path of my life, and if I would begin to learn to trust Him and lean on Him, I would experience success that could never again be taken away from me. He would open a door that no man could shut.

In addition, He could give me the favor I needed in order to advance in any realm of business. He could change the hearts of men. He could ensure a loan for advancement. If I would give Him the opportunity, He had the power, plan, and position to deploy my dream.

I hadn't gone to Him before this. I had looked to my friends at the corporate level. I had found comfort in Southern Comfort and friendship in Jack Daniels. But I hadn't sought God. Now all that was beginning to change, and so was my heart.

DESTROYED FOR LACK OF KNOWLEDGE

The Bible says that God's people are destroyed for lack of knowledge, and that is exactly what happened to me. I hadn't taken the time to learn about God, to become schooled in the power of His Word. I had never spent long hours hanging out with Him. I'd never come to know Him as a partner in business, a strategist in planning, or a genius in economics and finance.

So I invested my time during in this season of recovery rediscovering God, my faith, and the Bible. Learning about God would net some powerful results. I would begin to discover my purpose and my destiny in Him. God had created me for a purpose, and I needed to discover what that was in order to progress.

I learned that I had been called to go into the business world. I had been created to dominate and rule in the earth through business. Nevertheless, He operated differently than KFC and corporate America.

I had some catching up to do. So I immersed myself in the Word of God and prayer. I needed to know God. That became the passion of my soul, for I became intent upon maximizing my faith. For the first time in my life, I became intimate with Him.

Letting Your Light Shine

Instead of talking the talk, I begin walking the walk. The Bible tells us to let our light shine before men so that they can see God through our works. I took that verse to heart and started living it. I changed the way I dressed. As an unemployed person, I had fallen into the trap of dressing according to how I felt, and I had stopped shaving. So I had to clean myself up.

My eyes were open wide, and I realized that my yard was looking as unkempt as I was. So I mowed the grass, trimmed the hedges, and went on a campaign to repair everything around the house that I had neglected.

My heart was changing, and so was my environment. I dropped some of my toxic friendships, and people began to call me saying, "Jerome, where have you been? Let's go get a drink."

"Can't do that anymore. I've stopped drinking." For the first time in my life, I was completely committed to walking the walk. I was becoming a good steward according to God's design.

That's what building a relationship with God is all about. If your environment never changes, then you cannot hear God. When you're ready to move into a different realm, everything around you will look different, and you will, too. God will change everything about you from the inside out.

I also started to appreciate all that God had blessed me with, and my heart was changing even more. I was becoming genuinely grateful for my life and the blessings in it. I could begin to reassess according to wisdom. I didn't have a job, but I still had a great deal for which to be thankful. That sense of gratitude was activating the power of God in my spirit, because we enter in through thanksgiving. By activating faith, I was opening the door to my destiny, and I didn't even realize it.

THE EMPLOYMENT OF POWERFUL THOUGHTS

Thoughts do matter. And I began to realize that my self-pity and negativity were putting my mind in bondage and hindering my destiny. I began to think differently and speak differently. I became increasingly positive.

I was no longer thinking, *I can't do that. Woe is me! God, why does this have to happen to me?* My thoughts were changing. I was genuinely grateful, positive, affirming, and optimistic. My words reflected the new outlook and faith in my soul.

You will never maximize misfortune in your life if you chain down your soul and mind with negativity and self-pity. Positive, faith-filled words are empowered words, words that will open the doors to your destiny.

I began to speak into my ability. I declared: "I'm getting ready to own my own company." "I have the potential to go out and start a restaurant." I was feeling anticipation in my spirit. A breakthrough was coming my way. Yet in my mind I was still thinking that KFC was going to come back around. I started to speak those things that were not as though they were.

People had prophesied to me that KFC was going to call and ask me to come back. However, as time went on, I realized that that was not God's plan. Therefore, I changed my thought processes. I started FAITHS Incorporated (Finance and Investment Through the Holy Spirit), which was going to be the name of my restaurant. I declared that I had a restaurant company named Faith Incorporated. I was speaking from the unseen hoping for the seen, boldly declaring my faith and opening up the doors to my destiny. I planned to use Faith Incorporated as a mechanism of blessing into the kingdom of God. I was going to reach people and serve Jesus Christ in the realm of business.

RESURRECTING YOUR DREAM

I began to rediscover my dream. When I began to declare my potential, the dream of success that seemed dead came back to life. I remembered the success in realizing my dreams that God had given to me in the past. I had asked Him for a number of things, and had He given them all to me. He withheld nothing. Why wouldn't He empower me to realize my dream once more? Of course He would!

If you have a dream that has been dead, resurrect it. Remember the fulfillment of past dreams, of past visions. Remember your lion and your bear, as David did. When David was faced by a new giant named Goliath, he recollected giants he had slain before. The power of resurrection for your dream lies in your ability to remember and recollect previous victories. What God has already done for you, He will do again. Your spirit will grow stronger and bolder as you refuse to forget the miraculous victories of your past.

It occurred to me that God had given to me everything for which I had asked Him. My faith became bolder so that I was able to ask Him once more to fulfill my dream.

MAXIMIZING YOUR DREAM

I felt as though God was saying to me, "You laid hold of your dreams, but you didn't maximize those dreams. You grew content with what you achieved, and you stopped growing."

One of the most dangerous things that can happen to you is that you cease to grow. The wrong kind of contentment and satisfaction can cause you to refuse to go forward into the fullness of your destiny. That's what I had done. I became satisfied with the status quo of my life, not realizing that there were new levels for me to climb. God is not a God of comfort. He is a God of expectation of His will being done, and though many and great may be our plans, only His plans will survive.

DARING TO DREAM AGAIN

The day I sat on my basement steps and heard God speak to me, my response formed the seed to birth a new dream. I told God, "If you give me another opportunity, I will exalt You."

My new dream was to leave a legacy in this world. I started looking at the poverty mentality of the African-American race, our selfishness as a people. I looked at the folks using drugs and women selling their bodies. I would ride in my vehicle and see trash on the street, overgrown yards, and liquor stores located within a few blocks of churches. I began to see how we are manipulated and controlled by our own environment. All we see are drugs and alcohol.

Season of Change

My life was gaining a new sense of meaning, and I was emboldened by a fire and a passion to impact the African-American community. I had a new dream, a dream that involved maximizing the despair and poverty in our communities, maximizing the resources inside the people, and making a difference.

I was truly changed. I had maximized the failure and become a new man on the inside, filled with a new vision, new dream, and new destiny.

The First African-American Denny's Franchise Owner

A year and a half after I had been fired, I was spending a lot of time with God. I had prepared a place in the basement of my home where I could go and pray, read, and meditate day and night in His Word. For once in my life there were no distractions of work and responsibilities. It was at this time that I had a significant encounter with God and began a personal relationship with Him.

He was not a punisher of sinners who watched you for everything you did wrong. He was not a God that demanded you give to the church and never prosper. He wasn't even a God who disliked you if you wore certain clothing or makeup on Sunday. No, God was bigger than Sunday school and Sunday morning worship.

One day when I was in the basement, studying the Word of God, I happened to glance over at a magazine. The title was *Black Enterprise Magazine*, and on the front was a photo of a Denny's corporate executive with the president of the NAACP.

I took the magazine upstairs with me after I was finished with my study. The magazine fell open to an ad that said, "NAACP settles Fair Share Agreement with Denny's. If you're interested in becoming a franchisee for Denny's please send your information," and then listed the address.

My heart skipped a beat, and the Lord spoke to into my spirit, "Put your package together, *now*." So I put together all the articles that had appeared in newspapers about what I had accomplished at KFC, along with letters from the mayor and other notable public figures. I attached my resume and, after prayer, I took it to post office and marked it "priority mail."

Three days later they called me and flew me to their headquarters. I arrived not understanding that they had already decided to offer me the franchise. My final meeting was with the president of Denny's, Mr. Ron Petty. He said, "Jerome, we want you to make you the first minority franchisee to graduate from Denny's Minority Franchise Program. You'll own these Denny's restaurants. This will be your business, your company, and we'll take you through our program to ensure your success. After reviewing your credentials we have noticed a pattern of success, people skills, and tremendous qualifications, despite your abrupt termination from your previous employer. We have also noticed your ability to perform successfully in the African-American community, an area, as you know, in which we need tremendous help. If you're willing to teach us, we are willing to let you lead our national Minority Franchise Program."

Just like Joseph, who went from the pit to the palace, I went from being an unemployed man in my basement to becoming the nation's first African-American Denny's franchise owner graduate. God granted me a gift of success—the opportunity to maximize my dream. God could have simply given me a job, but he gave my heart's desire of being a restaurant owner. He could have made me just one of the minority franchise program graduates, but He made me the head and not the tail.

Now, let me share with you something that is far more important than achieving success in business. It is achieving success at home with your wife and family.

CHAPTER 7

MAXIMIZING FAVOR IN FAMILY

Meeting my wife was the best thing that ever happened in my life. I was twenty-one years old, and I didn't have a clue about what I was doing. Still, I saw someone, she looked good, and I went after her. In less than a year, I married her. Then I had to learn how to keep her, and I, or should I say we, had a lot to learn!

I met Alena right after I moved to Michigan to live with my uncle. She was working at the collection agency when I applied for a job there. Following my interview, I ran into her in the hallway, and I immediately thought she was truly fine.

"Do you work here?" I asked.

"Yes."

"Well, I just interviewed for a job. Do you think I'll get hired?"

She said, "I know they liked you because they were talking about you. I think you'll make it. I'll put in a good word for you."

Little did I know then that one of the first people I spoke with there would end up becoming my wife. I walked into that place and met my destiny.

MAXIMIZING DESTINY

It's amazing that we think that we're going in one direction, and all the while God is setting up our destiny in more ways than the human eye can see. Eyes that look are common, but eyes that see are rare. On that day I saw something in Alena that I wanted to spend a lifetime with, and as God said during creation, *It was good*. I had just left the military and moved to Michigan with my uncle. At the time, I felt that I had lost everything after my career in the military came crashing down around me. Yet it was all a part of God's sovereign plan for my life. My steps were being directed by God.

God's purpose for my going to that place was not for me to get a job, although they did hire me. My true purpose in going there was to find my helpmate, to meet my wife, the love of my life, the mother of my only children on Earth. Once I had thought that I lost everything when my basketball career ended. Then I felt that I had lost everything when my military career ended. But if I had not suffered these losses, I would not have come to the places where I could gain even greater things. Again and again in my life I've experienced loss, which is why I'm writing this book. The pattern that accompanied my losses became my gain as I learned how to maximize them. A key element in that was learning to see God's sovereign hand extended beyond the momentary pain. I had to learn to push forward, speed up recovery, and see past the hurt, pain, and confusion to something much greater: purpose and destiny.

The power to push past disappointments, deterrents, and misfortunes came from the fields of dreams. Looking up into that vast, starry sky every night convinced me deep down in my soul that there was something much greater, something beyond the conflicting and confusing circumstances of my life. Deep inside my soul I understood that my destiny and purpose lay beyond myself and beyond my understanding. My destiny was secure in the vast, sovereign plan and purpose of God. And that hand was at work again fulfilling the part of my plan called family.

MAXIMIZING FATHERHOOD

While I stayed with my Uncle Bill, I discovered him in new ways. He was the father I never had, the only father I ever had, and to this day I call him dad. I was excited and delighted to be there with the guy who used to drive into that dusty town with the shiny, new Cadillac, the one everybody looked up to and seemed to know.

It dawned on me that this was what I had prayed for so often: a father, a dad. How often had I looked into that night sky and asked God to let Uncle Bill be my dad? Suddenly, all the circumstances in my life had changed and that prayer was being fulfilled.

I went through an entire cycle of events—basketball, the military—and finally came back to exactly what I had prayed for. I had asked the Lord to allow me to have what Uncle Bill had, and now events were unfolding in my life that would bring that to pass.

Now I was realizing my destiny, the plan and purpose for my life that I had prayed about as a child walking those fields. A part of that destiny was my wife and future children, and Alena was right there, too. God does answer prayers, but if we rush through life impatiently and reck-lessly, not listening to the voice of God in the midst of our misfortunes, we will miss a season of change that fulfills our prayers. Don't be in a rush to pray away your storms; instead, began praying that you'll learn God's lesson from the trials, tribulations, and tests of authenticity.

It had always been one of my desires and one of my plans to have a wife and family. I deeply longed to prove myself by achieving something I had never had. Father and mother were missing components in my life, and the loss was deep and continual as I grew up. The only oppor-tunity in my life to experience parenting would be when I myself was a parent. Becoming a parent was extremely important for me, and now God had broken a genera-tional curse of poverty so that I could be more of a bless-ing to my family than I ever dreamed. Wow!

TESTING YOUR AUTHENTICITY

God knows the purposes and plans for your life. What we must learn is that obtaining God's promises requires that we undergo a process of change. You may see your life as a direct path, but God has many varying tests, tri-als, tribulations, and detours that you have to endure to prove yourself to Him. There are tests of authenticity that accompany the commitments you make to God to do a particular thing. Jesus was led into the wilderness to be tempted by the devil, to be tested for His authenticity.

After Jesus passed that test, His ministry (destiny) began. First He had to endure the tests and trials that proved and proofed Him, that strengthened Him, and that allowed Him to reveal all that was deep down inside Him.

In order to walk into purpose towards my destiny I had to prove myself to God. The life and legacy of my big brother and Savior, Yeshua, demonstrated that very pattern. Once He succeeded, once He passed through the trials, His ministry began. In life's misfortunes, I learned to count it all joy when I encountered trials, tests, and temptations.

As a very young man I had been tested, but those tests allowed me to realize one of my greatest dreams, that thing I asked for under a magnificent canopy of stars. I received my two sons, Aaron and William, and my daughter, Cherita.

MY DEFINING FACTOR

So what if you are fatherless or motherless? Why hurt as I did over something no one can control? Take control of your life and make sure your generation doesn't experience the same pain. My life and destiny were shaped by two people: my grandmother, who raised me, and my wife, who saved me and brought me to the throne of salvation.

Let me share with you a little more about those early years after I met Alena at the collection agency.

Alena and I began to date and eventually moved in together. However, our intimate relationship was getting the better of her conscience, for she was a committed believer. She began to talk to me about salvation, but I would always respond with, *I know many people in church who do the same things I do, so what's the difference?* I knew people who would stop by the drug dealer's house on the way home from church.

Back then my conscience was not that strong. One day, she announced, "We're not living like this any longer. We're not going to do anything that God has sanctified only for those who are in a covenant agreement with Him.

In other words, you're not going to touch me anymore until you give your life to Christ and our life to marriage."

Although I had prayed to God, I had never truly committed my life to Him and become a born-again believer. My experience on the mourner's bench really didn't count.

I had been challenging Alena's faith for some time. She'd ask me to go with her to church, and I'd refuse, saying, "Why go to church? You and I go out and party, and you go to church and I don't. At least the Bible says to be hot or cold. You're lukewarm." Man, we battled over that thing. "Look at you," I taunted. "You're staying here with me, and you call yourself a Christian?"

Finally, she agreed. She said, "Okay, you're right about all those things. We shouldn't be doing all of these things, because they are against my faith. I shouldn't be intimate with you outside of marriage. The Bible says we can't stay together and we can't have sex."

Suddenly, I realized that I had defeated my own purpose. I had talked Alena out of continuing the relationship that I so enjoyed. I started to panic.

"Well, I'm sorry, I apologize." I had talked myself into a corner.

She tucked her pretty hand against her hip and declared, "Well, you've got to go to church and get saved. That's the only way this can work."

Reluctantly at first, I went to church. But once I finally went forward to accept the Lord Jesus Christ as my personal savior, a dark cloud was lifted from my life. I remember leaving the church with my wife that day and rolling down the window of my car at every stoplight and yelling, "I'm saved! Hey, you on the street, I'm saved!"

My wife was laughing the entire way home at the joy she saw in me.

"You're crazy, Jerome," she said.

I said, "No, I am saved."

I told my neighbors, "Hey, I got saved today, man. I'm saved, and I know Christ." Right away, I was on fire for God and ready to learn all about this new faith walk. I was pumped up.

My salvation has been a key factor in my success in my personal life and my business life. I've discovered that all things really are possible to him who believes.

NEVER ABORT YOUR DESTINY

About that same time Alena discovered that she was pregnant. We had been living together and sharing the same car. At this time she was studying for an exam so she could begin working for a major airline, and at the same time I was transitioning to start my career in the fast food service industry. Often, she would drop me off at the collection agency and then go and study.

I've always had a thing about being late. I just hate to be late, and Alena understood that very well.

One day she was very late picking me up from work, and I was fuming. When she finally pulled up in the car, it was very obvious that she had been crying. Her face was swollen and wet with tears.

I got into the car and instantly my anger turned into concern. "What's wrong? Why are you crying?"

She said, "I'm pregnant, and I was going to get an abortion today. I wasn't going to tell you about it. But I couldn't go through with it, because I had to leave and come and get you because you were going to be late. I knew you were going to be mad about my being late."

I was stunned. I said, "You were going to kill my child? As much as I love children and you, and you were going to abort...?"

We already had a daughter and Alena didn't want to go down this path again unmarried. Heaving with sobs, Alena explained, "I don't want to have another child out of wedlock. I'm not going to do that anymore."

I said, "Well, then, I'll marry you."

Her crying stopped instantly, as if I had turned off a faucet. Disbelief filled her face, and she said, "What did you say?"

I took Alena's hand in mine, and whispered softly, "Alena, will you marry me? Let's raise our family together."

She started crying again, only now she was smiling at the same time.

Her parents threw us a big wedding and we got married. Many of my relatives, who once whispered to one another that I would never amount to anything, attended. The generational curses that they had cast over my life with their words had fallen powerless to the ground. Proudly, I walked down the aisle with my gorgeous bride and at the same time destroyed the generational curse of being fatherless that had plagued all my siblings' lives.

It was one of the best decisions of my life. Marriage to Alena has kept me out of a lot of trouble, and it has helped me to conquer the tests that would come. Without Alena, I don't know if I could have gotten through the difficulties, discouragement, and depression that accompanied getting fired from KFC.

Marriage was a giant step towards fulfilling my destiny and realizing the promise of my dreams. Had I aborted my desire to marry my wife—which I considered momentarily when I later got cold feet—or if we had aborted that child, I would have missed my destiny.

However, I passed the test, and Alena became a defining factor in my life. Marriage and family would turn out to be two of the greatest gifts in my life—and the greatest factors in maximizing my destiny. The power of God's favor and coming into covenant agreement, man's greatest tool for defeating life's storms, had become my portion.

IT MATTERS WHO YOU SLEEP WITH

The person Alena was, her kindness, patience, compassion, strength, and let me not forget courage and determination, helped to determine who I would become. I was first interested in her because she was beautiful. When we met she was modeling all over Detroit, and I was surprised and pleased that such a lovely woman could be interested in a country boy like me from Arkansas and Hermondale, Missouri.

But Alena wanted a man who would walk in the fear of God. Alena had been a believer for much longer than I, and she provided leadership in matters of faith and integrity, especially in those early years of our relationship. Without that leadership, I would not have gotten to where I am today. She was truly sent to me by God as my helpmate.

For once in my life I had companionship, I felt complete, and I had love for and from that special someone. We were building our life together, and Alena would prove to become a cornerstone of my strength and a supporting strength of our family.

MAXIMIZING CHILDREN

My mother didn't attend my wedding. Only God knows where she was and what she was doing.

Nevertheless, it was a very, very important day in my life—a new beginning of everything.

Several months later, my first son was born, and he was the joy of my life. Witnessing the seed that I produced, just holding him in the hospital and experiencing that miracle, I wondered, *Man, how, could anybody not want to be a part of this? I just duplicated myself.*

I would never abort my gifts, so we began to grow as a bonded unit, and my life had a new meaning—family. I was deeply moved inside by the sense of purpose I was experiencing. I was an adult, a family man, a parent, a father, and a husband, all at the ripe old age of twenty-two. My life was privileged with this new role of leadership and value.

You can goof up in college, goof up in the military, but when you're a father and a husband, you're in a real leadership role and it's serious business. At twenty-two, gaining a family was making me a man.

MAXIMIZING FAMILY

And so I made it my quest to be the best for my family, and I was determined. All my life I had wanted to experience life in a family, and now it was given to me. Family was a gift. Life as an individual ended and I started living my life for them—for my family.

I was determined that my family would have everything it needed to begin a new legacy of freedom. The generational curses of my past were going to be left behind in my children's generation—I would see to it. It was my turn for leadership in the family, and under my headship would come a paradigm shift. I was going to leave them an inheritance of wealth and kingdom-living knowledge. There would be an end to fatherless generations, an end to motherless generations, an end to poverty-stricken generations, and an end to alcohol- and drug-addicted generations.

The wounds were still fresh and raw from the words and curses spoken over me when I was growing up. The voices still rang in my head. *You're not going to amount to anything. You're nothing but a bastard child. Nothing good is going to come from those kids.*

I had spent my life fighting against those words, rejecting and refusing the sting of their impact. I maximized that pain; I took it and turned it into positive energy that fueled the passion in my soul for something more, for truth beyond the destructive lies spoken against my soul. My children would be the generation that would conquer, the generation that would go into the land of promise. They would never hear the lies, and they would never need to be healed from the scars.

I decided that, no matter what disagreements my wife and I might have, I would never walk out on my family. I would stay no matter what. Our covenant together would be continual and lasting, and our bonds would be strong. I would never leave my kids; only death would us part.

Those vows would be tested. Alena and I were very young and inexperienced. We had a lot of growing up to do together. And once after a blowup between us, I started to walk out. Alena reminded me of my vow, how I promised that I would never abandon my family. The pain of having parents who walked out on me reappeared and plagued me. I had a choice to stop the curse, even though it was costing me something temporarily. I turned around and never thought about walking away again. I stood my ground and made my choice, and I passed a major test of manhood.

Alena and I grew up together, and we spent our young life *together*. We mentored one another in times of joy and despair. We set standards for ourselves as a couple, as individuals, and for our family. We took the prospect of raising a family and overcoming the past very seriously. We maximized the pain and disappointments of the past, the brokenness, poverty, and loss. In so doing, we turned a new page for our future generations.

We didn't have a lot of outsiders impacting our lives together. We had one another, and we saw ourselves as a team. We were raising our family according to new standards, and we were blazing a new trail for ourselves and becoming an example to others.

MAXIMIZING THE COVENANT OF MARRIAGE PARTNERSHIP

Alena was my wife, my soul mate, and the woman of my life. We started as partners in family and we ended up becoming partners in business and in the work of the destiny of our lives.

In business, I've discovered that your wife can be your most valuable asset. She is the one who knows you best. She knows what makes you tick. She understands how you think and why you are doing the things you do. She can become your most powerful advocate or most vocal spokesperson.

Many businessmen leave their wives behind, kiss them goodbye when they go off to work, and never realize that they are leaving the most valuable asset of their business. They go out and hire someone who will represent them to their employees, but that individual may not have the loyalty, understanding, and insight of the wife they just kissed goodbye.

Your wife can also be your greatest encourager, your greatest strengthener—the only one who sees that you're feeling down or knows why something makes you happy. Your wife is your greatest gift, so learn to maximize that relationship in order to enjoy the full fruits of success it can bring to you.

When I was a franchisee at Denny's, I really wanted to expand the business. I had an opportunity to own as many Denny's restaurants as I wanted, but I had a problem finding the right business partners to make the endeavor a success. I tried to bring a number of people into partnership with me. It never worked, and they always seemed to have ulterior motives.

I later discovered that every night when I went home and went to bed I was sleeping next to the best business partner I ever had. Yet I had never capitalized on that relationship. I didn't maximize my marriage. Men who make the decision to leave their wives and children are absolutely insane.

I don't know what I'd do if I couldn't wake up in the morning and see my wife and my daughter and sons. Living in the favor of those relationships keeps me strong and encouraged. It's what life is all about. It's what drives me to want to become something more than I am.

My wife and I pray together every morning. She's the executive director and cofounder of Christian Business Network, Inc., my mentoring agency for entrepreneurs. She's the co-president of all my business endeavors. She's cosigner on all my bank and investment accounts. She's the one who helps to make it all come together, so that I'm able to impart something very meaningful to others. There's simply no way that I could have achieved all that I've been able to do without her. She's a tough, no-nonsense lady, who loves to have fun and helps me to make it all work.

Maximizing Your Good Thing

The Bible says that when a man finds a wife he finds a good thing. And that's what I've found with Alena— only good. She is my encourager, and her presence strengthens me. She knows how to build me up. She's my lover, my woman, and my friend. She's everything I need in a woman.

After we were married, I began to be built up by her encouragement. She would say, "Jerome, you know how to do so many things."

She would brag about me. "My Jerome can do anything! Jerome, there's nothing you can't do. When something breaks in the house, you're able to fix it. You always know what decisions to make. You seem to always know what to do."

She replaced the negative words that had been spoken all my lifetime with positive, strengthening ones. With her encouragement and kindness, I started to discover who I really was. I was not the dirt farmer who would never own his own land and could hope for little more than driving the truck every day. I was someone who could really achieve all that was in my heart to do. Somewhere under the canopy of her kind words I stopped being that bastard child and began thinking of myself as a successful businessman.

If you are a businessman or even a preacher, your success will come much more easily if you maximize the relationship of a good wife. Don't overlook one of the most valuable resources in your life.

My life was proving everyone wrong. Everyone who set up a standard of failure against me was being refuted. Shortly after our marriage, we were living far better than most of the people who had spoken such negative things about my life.

I began to gain a sense of inner peace and self-worth. As my soul mate pumped me up by speaking so many great things about me, things I had never heard previously, I was being strengthened internally.

I had a woman in my life to encourage me, push me forward, and love me. Just that statement alone, *I love you,* had the power to bring out so much that was in me.

As a young husband and father, I looked around and saw what others around me were becoming. I made a decision that I wanted to become something more in life as well. I wanted my own slice of the American pie. I wanted to be successful, and because my wife believed in me I began to believe in myself as well.

We men aren't always the smartest individuals in the world. God created us and He decided that we needed some help. Realize that if you're going to be in a position to help someone, you might have to be smarter than he or she is. If you're a computer technician, you are hired to fix a computer, so you have to be smarter than that computer in order to fix it.

If you are a helpmate, then naturally you're smarter than the mate you're to help. If you're a wife, you may well be a little smarter in some ways than your husband. God designed it to be that way, so you could help the brother out. Nevertheless, you don't have to go around trying to be the boss. Rather, come up with constructive ways to help him and your reward will be the desires of your heart. Ask my wife, if you run into her at one of the numerous malls around the world.

MAXIMIZING THE FAVOR OF GOD AND FAMILY

I had started on the fast track program of management at KFC, kissing my wife goodbye in the morning and dropping off our children at day care. As I began to realize that I was already achieving success in much of what I had only dreamed of, that passion for success was fueled inside of me even more.

After getting married, I began to realize that I was walking in a greater sense of God's favor in my life. That covenant relationship at home was producing good fruit in me.

Although I couldn't put it into words, I knew within myself that I was going to become successful in life. I began to seize and maximize every moment in my life in pursuit of that goal. I was moving forward in becoming who God called me to be.

TWO ARE BETTER THAN ONE

The Bible says that two are better than one, because if one falls down the other can help him up (see Eccles. 4:9). During my time of unemployment, my wife proved the truth of this passage. I was out of work for a year and a half, and she spent that time working double shifts to help us make ends meet. When I stumbled in drunk, I would wake up to find her washing my face with a warm washcloth and playing soft worship music in the background while she prayed.

She told me later that when she no longer knew what to do with me, she decided she knew my Creator. She went back to Him, and told Him that since He created me, He had to know how to fix me. She prayed for me continually.

THE STAR OF PROMISE

I had looked for that star of promise in the sparkling sky night after night as a child. But I discovered a real star when I married my wife. Her favor has been a shining star in my life that has pointed the way to my destiny.

On one of the happiest days of our lives, I sent a letter to the airlines she worked for and told them that I appreciated the time they had given her to hone her success skills. However, effective immediately she would be resigning to become a business owner. We would be working together from now on as successful business owners, the managers of multiple food service operations and other ventures, including the best youth and entrepreneurial training center in America, the Christian Business Network.

I ended the letter with, "Thank you for the eleven years that my wife has spent at your corporation. But due to my recent successes, she will no longer be employed for your organization, for I am going to take care of her for the rest of her life."

CHAPTER 8

MAXIMIZING THE TRUTH IN CHANGE

Self-discovery and change are keys to success at anything you want to do in life. The misfortune of the year and a half of unemployment I underwent taught me a great deal about who I was and how I could change.

Your inability to become who God has called you to be affects other people.

The Bible says, "But prove yourselves doers of the word, and not merely hearers who delude themselves. For if anyone is a hearer of the word and not a doer, he is like a man who looks at his natural face in a mirror; for once he has looked at himself and gone away, he has immediately forgotten what kind of person he was. But the one who looks intently at the perfect law of liberty, and abides in it, not having become a forgetful hearer but an effectual doer, this man shall be blessed in what he does" (Jas. 1:22-25, NAS).

I had learned the spirit of application, the ability to discern and apply kingdom principles to my everyday life.

I studied and applied them to show myself approved not by man but by God. I had, for the first time in my life, graduated from dependence on people.

The Word of God will show you who you are and how you need to change in order to succeed. You may want to start your own business, launch your own ministry, or embark upon another endeavor that will define you. But before you can do that you must begin to know you—you must discover who you are according to God's truth, not the blindness that comes from the human ego.

If you don't know who you are before you launch out, it can kill you. I'm an athlete, a college All-American from Arkansas State University. Many of my friends are also professional sportsmen—the NBA basketball players Rick Mahorn, John Long, and Terry Mills, and the NFL's Troy Vincent and Reggie White. Some men go into business as professional athletes at nineteen, and start making millions of dollars. We've all read about what happens to some of these athletes. As young men, they lack wisdom regarding their wealth. They are foolish and making millions, which allows them to finance their foolishness at its highest level. This wasn't the case with any of the NBA and NFL friends I mentioned, but they had seen it in some of their peers.

Having wealth and not knowing the correct way to use it is a dangerous situation to be in. You've got to be careful what you ask God for, because you may get it and not know what to do with it. You could end up spending the rest of your life trying to undo the damage you created by not being prepared for success. You could be a millionaire but end up in prison, like the boxer Mike Tyson.

Instead of going down in history as the greatest basketball player that ever walked the planet, you're remembered for beating your wife or committing adultery.

Instead of being known as the king of rock music, you become the king of child molestation.

You've heard of the wages of sin, but you must fully understand that sin will truly pay you. You might think you're getting away with something, but nobody ever does. Sin will pay you its wages, and those wages will be waiting for you when you wake up to the truth of what you've been doing.

It's absolutely essential that you understand these things if you're going to grow in business. There are certain things that can stop you dead in your tracks or keep you from getting in the door in the first place. The Bible says that if you do certain things, you cannot enter into the kingdom of God. Certain activities and behaviors will keep your prayers from reaching heaven, so praying becomes useless. If you get up in the morning, get on your knees and pray, and then go out and take part in sexual immorality, pornography, deviancy, lust, cheating, lying, and other sinful behaviors, your prayers will have no meaning.

You may be wondering why your blessings haven't come. Have you considered the truth in change in your life? Have you looked at yourself in the cold truth of Scripture and asked God to change you into the man or woman He created you to be? Life is a choice, so my prayer for you this day is to choose life and its attributes.

MAXIMIZING THE TRUTH OF SELF-DISCOVERY

During those long months when I was unemployed, I discovered who I was. Even though I was a male, I wasn't the man God had designed me to be. While I had been rising to a high level of success at KFC, I had been neglecting my position in my family. Not having a father as I grew up left me without the knowledge of what a man's role as a father really meant. A man would not neglect his family or his home. A man would not accept unwise counsel during trials. A man would be a loving husband and father whether he was employed or unemployed. I hadn't been living as a role model and a leader of influence. I was operating in fear principles, not godly principles.

Therefore, I had to rediscover what it meant to be a man, what being a man was all about. A man takes care of his home. A man doesn't cause his wife to work double shifts while he sits at home saying, "Woe is me!" Even though God was perfecting me and destroying the spirit of pride in my life, I felt useless.

As I went through the process of self-discovery, I rediscovered that I was somebody. I had lost my job, but that did not mean I had no skills or abilities. I had taken a restaurant concept nationwide, impacting five hundred stores. I had achieved the highest volume of sales and profits in the nation. I was able to develop and train more store managers and assistant managers than anyone in the company had before.

This period of unemployment did not mean that I was a failure. It meant that I needed time to rediscover myself. I had to gain a sense of self that was not inflated by pride and ego, but was honest and real in the light of truth.

I also realized that God's favor was upon my life. I have an anointing upon my life to do business, to build relationships, to encourage people, and to help them get to the next level. I left the company believing that it had made me, but I was learning that God had placed abilities and gifts within me long before I was employed by KFC.

It was my work ethic, my skills, my sweat equity, my destiny, my purpose in life—and all those things were already inside me, able to be activated at levels I had never before imagined. All I needed to do was to build a relationship with the person who created me in order to get there.

WHO YOU ARE AND WHOSE YOU ARE

I discovered that my success in business wasn't about Jerome. You see, self-discovery is not only about who you are, but whose you are, which is even more important. When I discovered who I was and whose I was, I realized that this whole matter of self-discovery is not about Jerome. It's about God, and it's about letting my light shine so that people will see my good works though Him operating in me. It's about becoming the person God intended me to be when He created me, and then allowing that person to be seen.

As I said earlier, success involves becoming the person you were destined to be and fulfilling your destiny. Success has little to do with accomplishing your own plans, but everything to do with allowing God to accomplish His plans through you.

I always had lots of plans but never achieved true success until I started walking in God's counsel, His plan, and His purpose for my life. According to my good friend and mentor, Dr. Myles Munroe, becoming a leader involves understanding and developing your untapped potential in God.

To achieve your own success, ask yourself: Why are you here? Why did God create you? What are you called to do? Where in the world are you going?

When I first attempted to answer those questions for myself, I realized that I didn't have a clue as to why God had placed me here on earth. I didn't know who I was, so how could I know where I was going?

If you don't know who you are in life, then any road will take you where you're going, and for me that was nowhere. I was ready and willing to jump on any road that rose up before me.

The Lord gave me a vision about how to travel the path before me. In the vision, He said, "Here you are, Jerome. Wide is the path to sin and unrighteousness, but narrow is the path to righteousness." Then He said, "On this path, Jerome, are left and right turns, and I've given you the direction. The way that you're supposed to go is very clear before you. But those turns are going to be very attractive. Those turns involve popularity, vanity, selfishness, people with big names, high-profile folks, and lots of worldly possessions. When you take those paths, you veer off a path of righteousness. Those other pathways lead to death."

It takes faith to stay on the narrow path. God said, "Don't be afraid of the unseen, for this path will sometimes take you into places that seem impossible to pass through. But don't worry, because if you walk with Me on this path you'll discover who you are. It's a process of growth, but if you make the decision to stay on the path, then you'll make it."

Today, I'm on the narrow path. If I ever veer off the path by taking it all for granted, then all I have to do is repent and God will place me back on it.

DISCOVERING YOUR SPIRITUAL EXISTENCE

I discovered that I was a spiritual being who was having a human experience, rather than a human being having a spiritual experience. I wasn't just a man on the face of this earth, here for the sake of making myself happy. I was a spiritual being.

I was created as an image of my heavenly Father. Because I was living in a relationship with God, I was one of the most powerful people on the face of the earth, with the ability to change the world.

HUMILITY, PRIDE, AND EGO

Your power to build a kingdom business enterprise will be driven by your ability to remember where you came from. That takes genuine humility. Pride has a stride, and it has a tendency to forget. It forgets about the weak, sick, endangered person that God picked up on the side of the road. And it can also forget God.

Pride comes before a fall, according to the Bible. Pride also is a type of spiritual blindness that results from losing touch with the reality of who you are and where you came from. Ego is little more than a mind that is blinded by pride, so never walk in your ego. Walk in humility and the gentleness of Christ. Pride and ego will destroy you, but humility will exalt you. God gives grace to the humble. Therefore, stay humble by maintaining your memory of how far God brought you and where you could be without Him.

Deuteronomy 8:18 tells us that God humbled us in order to give us the power to get wealth. In this passage of the Bible, God also warns us to remember where we came from and who we were when He helped us.

When you read the Bible, words such as *remember* and *but* are attention-getters. To those He had led out the wilderness, God said, "And you shall remember all the way which the Lord your God has led you in the wilderness these forty years, that He might humble you, testing you, to know what was in your heart, whether you would keep His commandments or not. And He humbled you and let you be hungry, and fed you with manna which you did not know" (Deut. 8:2-3, NAS).

We were poor growing up in the backwoods of Missouri-Arkansas state line, but I can't remember one time that we went without food to eat. We may not have had the finest home or clothing, but manna was always on our dinner table.

Never forget who you are without God. If you have a good memory, you'll be successful for a long, long time. If you maximize these truths in your life, you will never fail.

CHANGE AND AN ERA OF UNCERTAINTY

Since the attacks of September 11, 2001, everything in our economy is changing, and may continue to change for some time. Terrorism, corporate scandals, and the threat of war are rocking our economy. Businesses are reluctant to invest. The federal budget has gone from surplus to deficit, and the country has plunged into a war costing billions with no end in sight. The headlines are telling us that across this country, in corporate boardrooms and family living rooms, there is a sense of fear about what looms ahead. We are living in an era of greater uncertainty than our generation has ever experienced.

Change seems completely unavoidable. Nothing is as permanent as change. But should change be viewed as a negative thing?

DON'T MISS YOUR SEASON FOR CHANGE

When I first heard these words about change, they transformed my life. Change is natural to our existence and common to creation. Everything around us is in a constant state of change. Your own body is changing as you sit there and read. The cells that make up your body today will be completely regenerated in a few years' time.

Everything is in a state of change and nothing can stop it. Change is the evidence that you exist, that you are alive, and that your life is making a difference in the world around you. Don't let change alarm you, and never let the fear of change shut you down. Change is inevitable. It is a principle of creation; everything changes.

Accepting the inevitability of change in your life can bring tremendous peace and understanding to your existence. If we accept the inevitable truth that nothing remains the same and everything will change, we can minimize our level of expectations and disappointments.

In life, three types of changes define the patterns of our growth cycles:

- those that happen to us,
- those that happen around us,
- and those that we make happen.

There are also three types of change agents that you will encounter in this world:

- those who watch things happen,
- those who make things happen,
- and those who wonder what happened.

Which one are you? Which change agent are you? I'm committed to becoming a change agent. How about you?

Why were you born? Why where you placed upon this earth? Was it to change things? Was it to make things happen? Each one of us is here for different and multiple reasons. One of the reasons you may be here, living in this earth in this present time, is to become a change agent in your family, your church, your business or workplace, and your community.

If you believe in your vision enough to work for it, stand for it, and fight for it, then you are a change agent. You were placed on this earth to effect change. You're here to make things happen. If nothing's happening in your life, you should feel totally uncomfortable.

MANAGING CHANGE: THE ART OF BALANCE

If you reflect upon the matter, all of life is about balance. Good health is about balance. You must eat a good balance of the right foods in order to stay healthy, and you need to balance exercise with more sedentary tasks. Finances are about balance, too. The money you spend must be balanced with the money you take in. Family is a balancing act. If you spend too little time with the members of your family, the delicate balance of relationships gets off. Long trips away must be balanced with extra amounts of time together.

Change is a balancing act, too. If you are called as a change agent, you must learn the delicate art of balancing beneficial change in the lives of others with their perceived fear of losing comfortable norms. Changes enacted too hastily or too radically can have devastating consequences on the very people God has called on you to help.

Being a change agent is similar to becoming an artist. Successful change is an art form. Change can be a welcome blessing when it is achieved through balance, sensitivity, and care.

Never be so committed to a particular change that you forget who the change is for. Change is for people, and they must be brought to accept that change for it to work well. Never run over people in an effort to effect change. Without learning the art of balance, you will not be successful in accomplishing the change you seek.

A wise pastor of a large church decided he was going to change the form of worship there, and his first desire was to get the piano off the platform and replace it with more contemporary instruments. Over the course of an entire year he moved the piano a couple of inches every Sunday, until finally the piano was offstage.

When asked about the slow-moving piano, he said, "People can deal with any kind of change, as long as it's only an inch at a time."

This man understood the art of balance, and he was successful in changing the style of worship in his church without upsetting the worshipers. If you are called to be a change agent, learn how to manage change through the art of balance.

BE A CHANGE AGENT

The changes that we enacted at the KFC restaurants were innovative and creative. We got creative with the menu and offered our urban customers side dishes like the ones they ate with their home-cooked chicken dinners, and our sales skyrocketed. We sold chicken from drive-through windows during late-night hours. We cleaned up the stores and exterminated roaches and rats.

We took chances and dared to make bold changes. We saw what needed to change, and we moved to enact those changes within the confines of our budget and resources.

We were stewards of management, continually overseeing and enacting new, different, and bold changes.

We didn't just focus on corporate business; we raised money and empowered the communities in which we operated. We gave away scholarships, sponsored youth sporting events, and provided the high schools with role models of a better tomorrow. We were determined to change the status quo, and these changes spread to other urban business leaders across the country.

I went to the corporate players and I fought for change. I went to them and said, "Listen, in our neighborhoods we don't eat coleslaw and macaroni salad with our chicken. We like greens, macaroni and cheese, sweet potato pie, cornbread, and barbecued chicken."

They thought I was crazy, and told me, "Jerome, you need to stick to what we do as an organization. This is our standard. Follow it and stay in the box."

They told me I couldn't do it. Little did they know that my destiny is to be a change agent. I can't be made to conform to an environment, and I can't be controlled by those who want to protect the status quo.

Despite their disapproval, I made the changes. I broke out of the box, and the president of the entire company visited my restaurants. He saw the greens and barbecued chicken we were serving. My director of operations pulled me over to the side and I thought he was going to fire me for insubordination.

However, even he was shocked when the president of the company said, "This is awesome! This is how we should help move the brand in segment communities." As I've mentioned, that change, that innovation, went into more than five hundred restaurants nationwide.

Passing the Test as a Change Agent

There's a price to be paid if you've been called as a change agent. The paradigm will shift, and change will come, but those who bring that change will also pay a price for it. If you believe you're called to bring change, be fully aware that it will not come cheap and it won't be easy, but it will be worth it when it comes.

Even if you have to endure, just wait. The change you're expecting may not come when you project it will, but it's always right on time.

If you want to bring change, then you're going to be tested. You've got to pass that test and endure the moment in order to reap the lasting rewards.

When I realized that I was called by God to be a change agent, I gave up my Denny's and A&W franchises and became one hundred percent committed to Christian Business Network. I was called by God to empower men and women to launch themselves as entrepreneurs, take ownership in businesses, and become change agents in their own environments.

God's counsel stepped in and He put Christian Business Network as a burden on my heart. It's a burden of responsibility and calling from God, but it is also something that I deeply enjoy, because it's what I'm made to do. I'm not looking for a platform from which to speak. I'm looking for a generation for which God has called me to make a change.

What that means to me personally is that at three or four o'clock in the morning, when everyone else is sleeping in their beds, I might be up working, preparing, organizing, and investing all that I am into this effort. There's a price to be paid to become a kingdom change agent.

I might get a total of five hours of sleep in five days, but I'm still not tired. Serving your purpose is the most exciting position you can ever occupy. Once you discover your purpose, the passion of life becomes contagious. My calling as an entrepreneurial and economic empowerment change agent motivates me, stimulates me, and keeps me moving forward when my body wants to quit. I only have to look out and see the impact that God is having on people through my actions to get all charged up again. I'm fired up because I know what my destiny is and I'm walking in it, not tomorrow, but right now.

I look out at my classrooms filled with future entrepreneurs, and I know deep inside that those men and women have the power to change their neighborhoods and effect change in the entire world.

Jesus Christ brought change to the entire world by empowering just twelve individuals. Christian Business Network is touching hundreds and thousands of lives. If you want to be someone who can bring change to your generation, I encourage you to seek the greatest change agent: Yeshua Ha Maschia, Jesus the Christ. He can change and empower you to change others.

CHAPTER 9

MAXIMIZING THE RESOURCES OF NETWORKING

As you know, I was raised as a country boy from a town right on the state line between Arkansas and Missouri. Let me break down what that means. I lived on a gravel road, on Route 1, Box 110A. In order to know when the school bus was coming we would watch for a giant cloud of dust rising high in the air. When we saw the dust we'd run and shout to the other children, "Bus is coming, y'all! Come on...the bus is coming!"

Giant fields of white cotton surrounded our little wooden shack, and every year I earned money for school clothes by chopping cotton. I always found the process of farming amazing. At the beginning of the year the fields were bare and dead. The farmer would come out and till the ground, loosening the dirt so seeds could grow in it. Later he'd flatten the dirt, making it smooth for the plow. Then the seed planters would come, first creating rows with one kind of plow, and then using another to sow the seeds in the carefully-prepared ground. When the rain came, those once-dead seeds sprouted and broke forth from the dirt.

The farmers would stand out in the wind chewing straws, smelling the scent of the rain. At that point they knew that the harvest was on its way, for God was changing the season.

Every day the cotton plants grew taller, and soon it would be time for us, the field hands, to chop the weeds that grew among the cotton. If we didn't go through the fields and pull out the weeds and vines, or tares, then those wild plants would stunt or kill the farmer's crop.

Eventually, harvest time would arrive, and the big farm equipment would reap the harvest, some sixtyfold, some eightyfold, some a hundredfold, according to our good work in preparing the fields and ridding them of the enemies of growth. But do you know what happened if the farmer didn't harvest those fields on time? That vast gold mine of cotton would fall to the ground and rot. The entire harvest would be ruined because the laborers had not gathered it while it was in season.

Who or what have you allowed to stunt your growth and cause you to not reap a hundredfold in your season? How many seasons have you allowed the harvest that God predestined for you to be passed on to the wicked? I am convinced that your wealth, or lack of it, is hidden in your inability to recognize your season of change.

THE HARVEST IS RIPE IN OUR COMMUNITIES

I'm proud of my African-American heritage. I'm convinced that the African-American community is the backbone of this country. If every African-American took

Martin Luther King Day off, the nation's commerce would completely shut down.

I'm not preaching a black message, but I'm attempting to make a point. As African-Americans, we should be proud of who we are. I'm very proud of our culture. Nevertheless, as a race we must understand that if anyone is responsible for what's happening in our communities, it's us. Our communities are our responsibility.

I'm convinced that when you see prostitutes selling their young bodies on the street, drug dealers offering their illegal wares, and so many of our young men and women locked in prison, it's because our harvest is falling to the ground and rotting. It's because we failed to identify our purpose while it was in season.

THE HARVEST OF OUR COMMUNITIES

Drug dealers, prostitutes, and other young folks who are in prison systems across the world are the harvest of our communities. They are the harvest that has fallen to the ground and rotted, because we have not labored to prepare it, tend it, and bring it in.

How many of us will be held accountable on Judgment Day? How many of us were supposed to share a word, but were too busy minding our own business? How many of us felt compelled to go out and make a difference, but pulled back in fear, self-absorption, or self-interest?

That harvest has been watching us, examining our lifestyle, and walking in the example we've set. We take our remote controls and turn on CNN, and we become spectators watching young Pookie being hauled off to jail and Jordan robbing another store.

The harvest is ripe, but we, the laborers, are few.

MAXIMIZING COMMUNITY EMPOWERMENT

As a culture, we must stop being spectators and begin maximizing the resources of our communities in order to save our harvest. We must break the generational curses of the past and turn around the future of our next generation.

Much of the leadership from the 1960s Civil Rights movement no longer represents the African-American communities. Instead, "civil rights" has become a multi-million dollar business that exists by keeping racism alive, rather than by moving forward and empowering the next generation with the numerous corporate opportunities it wins. Because our leadership has not made this progression, and we have not stepped up and taken our own place, our harvest is rotting.

How much of the funding of that leadership from the Civil Rights era has been channeled back into our communities to help our citizens launch businesses, set up schools, build hospitals, and develop programs? The funds have poured into civil rights organizations by the millions—I know that as fact from my experience with Denny's. However, the harvest of young people that those millions of dollars were supposed to benefit have not been stewarded properly, and the destructive results are rotting on the ground because those resources are not empowering lives.

Meanwhile, personal glorification fuels the disease of racism. Much of the leadership exists to empower itself, and has lost its mission, which was to empower the communities that continue to suffer.

How much investment capital have African-American civil rights organizations provided to communities so that their people can launch independent businesses? Answer this question only after comparing it to the Jewish,

Catholic, and other organizations that have won billions of dollars in congressional funding to develop national programs. How many buildings have been erected with the so-called discrimination payout funds in our communities? How many ventures have been birthed from investing the millions of dollars that have been won through civil rights lawsuits? How many young people that you know have gone to college as a result of those funds? I have personally not met one, and I have traveled to many places. How many hospitals and treatment centers for the sick have been erected in our communities with money received from the health care industry? How many schools have been built? How many training centers? How many institutions? How many office buildings? Where are those vast resources going? What do we see as a result of those billions of dollars at the community level?

That leadership has set itself up as an echelon of elitism, not unlike that elitism that the leaders of the original Civil Rights movement despised. Our current leadership came into power based on its charges of being disenfranchised from the system. But it has not enfranchised the communities it purports to serve. Instead, it has continued the disenfranchisement by empowering itself while the harvest continues to rot and suffer.

The leaders fight for opportunities to get on television before corporate America to manipulate it into giving more and more funds that they then only spend their own efforts to maintain power. All the while, urban communities deteriorate more and more. There's more and more death, destruction, and mayhem, and more and more dissolution of the African-American communities. I've visited the urban communities in Atlanta where the streets are named after some of these great leaders, and they are the worst communities in the state. When did getting your name on a street become more important than revitalizing the community that bears your name?

I'll probably receive a lot of criticism for communicating these truths, but someone has take a stand and challenge these powerful proponents who prostitute our race for their own personal, unethical gain. If the shoe doesn't fit, don't wear it. If you don't like the truth, then help change it.

I believe it's time to make a change. But that change will only occur when we, as individuals, step up to the plate and take back our positions of authority in big business and in our communities. As individuals, we must make the necessary changes. The harvest is great, but the economically empowered laborers are few. There are two types of people who currently serve our urban communities: those who desire but don't have, and those who have and don't desire. Which one are you?

MAXIMIZING THE PURPOSE OF WEALTH

It takes more than resources to effect change. It takes resources that are used properly. Until that happens, change will not come and our harvest will continue to rot.

The African-American communities have wealth. Why do we have to depend upon the government to come in and give us food stamps, when we have many highly successful people in our communities? Too often when we begin to acquire wealth, we stop thinking in terms of community, or we may never have thought in terms of community at all.

Communities with a sense of identity have historically achieved success as a group, while communities without that sense have not. Certain European groups came into this country with the understanding that all boats rise with the tide. The Italians, the Irish, and a host of other ethnic communities were well-known for economically empowering individuals within them. Those groups saw communities as a resource. Although an individual immigrant might not have the funds to start a barbershop or a grocery store, he could, as a member of his community, find the necessary funding from the community as a whole.

Today, Jewish communities continue to provide one another with interest-free loans. If you live in one of their communities and want to start a business, you can find the funding you need to get started within the community. If you come into their community, you must also live by their code. If you don't, then you are isolated from the community, and you are marked and no longer able to operate within their system. You can no longer do business within their community.

MAXIMIZING RESOURCES

African-Americans live in communities, but we don't maximize our communities as a resource. In addition, we also don't maximize the other resources that we have.

We fuel our cars at gas stations we don't own, eat at restaurants we don't own, shop at thrift stores we don't own, and get our nails done in salons we don't own. If we don't own these places, then how can we reinvest dollars back into our community? We have become the most prominent buying industry in the world, with a national buying power of over $450 billion a year. However, less than two percent of this money is reinvested in our communities.

Our people form a major part of the workforce in this country. If all African-Americans stopped working for a single day, the country would shut down. We are restaurant cooks, airline baggage handlers, bank cashiers, and cab drivers. We are a wealth of human resources.

In addition, African-Americans are some of the most spiritual people on the face of the earth, but we don't apply that power. We have a form of godliness, but deny its strength. We don't maximize the power and potential of our religious experience. Neither do we maximize the power and potential our churches hold in our communities. Irish communities advanced rapidly because the church assisted its citizens in a host of ways, such as providing business loans, employment opportunities, and community services, and creating cultural and religious organizations. Our churches provide a great source of spiritual comfort and strength, and yet they are positioned to do so much more.

It is incorrect to say that African-American communities do not have money. We shout hallelujah, speak in tongues, and spend all our money on suits, watches, clothes, earrings, makeup, and cars. We look the part of people with worldly success, and then we go back to our own suffering environment.

I can drive through dilapidated neighborhoods and see people coming from churches who are dressed to a tee. The kids are wearing $200 gym shoes. When Michael Jordan came out with a new line of gym shoes, they sold out, and it was black folks out there purchasing them.

Don't tell me that we don't have money. We do. The philosophy, the thinking, the church—all of our experiences and our shepherds have not taught our people how to maximize our wealth so that it can empower us—work for us—as individuals and as a community.

MAXIMIZING YOUR OWN RESOURCES

God works through people. He is not going to come down in a cloud and give you everything you need. Scripture says, "Give, and it will be given to you; good measure, pressed down, shaken together, running over, they will pour into your lap" (Lk. 6:38, NAS).

In 2001, we launched our NxLevel Entrepreneur Training Institute. In our first class was a single mother who did not have transportation. Still, she made it to class every week on time by catching a bus from downtown, bringing her two children with her. She was determined to become a business owner.

One day, it occurred to me that I had a car that I hadn't used for months sitting in front of my house. I thought about selling the car, but immediately the Holy Spirit brought this single mother to mind. At the next class I gave her that car. After sixteen weeks, Lolita Davis graduated as our class valedictorian, and she is now a successful entrepreneur.

Because I gave that car to someone who needed it, a Jewish friend of mine gave me a new Mercedes-Benz, fulfilling the Scripture "give and it shall be given to you, good measure, pressed down, shaken together, running over." Every significant thing that I have ever accomplished in life was birthed through an act of unselfishness giving.

What God gives into your life, He does through people. The King James Version says, "shall men give into your bosom" (Lk. 6:38, KJV). That means that God will direct people in your life to give into your lack.

Do you know how many people God has brought into your life to take you to the next level? You may not even have shared your plans with them. You may have allowed the opportunity to pass you by simply giving them a handshake and moving on. You were not focused on the things of God.

Perhaps you didn't have the confidence to step out and try to start that business. You didn't have the faith to believe that you would have favor with that individual. You lacked enough information, or you lacked knowledge. When the person who was supposed to help you came along with all the resources you needed, you couldn't go forward because you weren't at the right place yet. You weren't ready. You weren't able to maximize that contact. That season passed you by, and you did not reap the harvest hidden in that source.

Today you may be struggling, and yet the resources that would have made the difference came across your path. You simply weren't prepared, and never identified the opportunity. You were not actively seeking God so that you had the sensitivity required to identify His provision when it came your way. You didn't maximize the opportunity you had.

Success is when preparation meets opportunity. One of the biggest reasons we're not prospering is that we're not prepared. Seasons are predestined by God; they do not arise from our own sense of timing. According to the United States Small Business Administration, statistics show that an average of seventy-five percent of all small businesses fail in their second or third year because of failure to plan or prepare.

The Bible says that God's people are destroyed for lack of knowledge. Your struggle today may be the result of not understanding, of not having enough knowledge to realize that the resources you needed were made available to you through someone with whom you were in contact. God sent someone to you, but you didn't maximize the opportunity.

How many hands have you shaken in your lifetime? Every one of those handshakes represents an opportunity. How many opportunities have you passed up? How many relationships were sent to you to create a network of power to enable you to achieve something that you could not do alone? God works through people called resources, so always be prepared to maximize yours.

MAXIMIZING THE PURPOSE OF WEALTH

You have far more wealth than you realize. The poorest American citizen ranks in the top percentile of the world's wealth. Sit down and count up how much wealth has gone through your hands in your lifetime thus far. It will surprise you. If you are forty years of age and have made an average income of $45,000 a year, you are a millionaire. The question is, did you invest your talents properly?

The reason people don't maximize the wealth that comes into their lives is because they don't know what to do with wealth once they have it. They have no purpose for that wealth beyond consumption.

If you have a vision, if you have a plan for a business, a ministry, or a financial endeavor, I guarantee you that not only will you maximize your own wealth, you will also begin to receive more.

Money will come to support your vision. All the resources you need to achieve your vision are out there waiting for you to rise up and take your place. First, you must maximize the purpose of wealth in your life. God will send the resources your way when you have a need that's beyond your own personal consumption.

Business people, I'm going to share with you how to become wealthy. It's simple. The Word of God says, "It is

He who is giving you power to make wealth." The next phrase is vitally important: "that He may confirm His covenant" (Deut. 8:18, NAS).

God does not give you wealth so that you can go out and spend every dollar you make and then some. You should pray about the money you receive. It's His money, not yours. You can't just spend God's money indiscriminately, in any way you want.

Sometimes you find out that the wealth has ended and you wonder why. It may have ended because you didn't spend it properly. You bought things that you lavished upon yourself, and you forgot about the reason for wealth. You never thought about using the money coming to establish God's covenant on earth.

I went a couple of years without buying any suits because I already had more suits in my closet than I could wear. New suits might have looked more stylish, but I didn't need them. I'm not suggesting that God doesn't want you to look good. But your desires must take second place to establishing God's covenant, to building what God has given you to build.

I have a friend in Dallas named Comer Cottrell who gives away millions of dollars, because he truly understands money. He says that the purpose of money is to give it away. He'll tell you that he gives money away because he likes helping people. It's his passion. He says that he likes making money because he likes helping people. And we wonder why the rich get richer? By the way, Comer is not even a tongue-talking, Bible-reading believer, but he is still leading most of you as a believer in God's purpose for wealth. We can learn a lot from the world.

We know the Bible in and out, and you ought to see us in church chanting, "Money cometh now to me." We say it until we're worn out, and yet money hasn't come. Why? Ask yourself, "Why is my money not coming to me now?"

One reason is that every time we need it, we need it now. You know why you don't have it now? You couldn't handle it now. You aren't ready now. If God blessed some of us with a great deal of money right now, it wouldn't profit us and we wouldn't profit others. That money wouldn't mean anything more than a new mink coat or a Mercedes-Benz. It wouldn't profit a cause higher than self.

When I was purchasing my building for Christian Business Network, I had to renovate the side of the building. I was praying, *Lord, Father, You gave me this building. Therefore, I know You're going to give me the money necessary to make these repairs. Just show me the resources.*

You need to believe that the money's out there for your cause. The resources are available. You're not broke. Stop praying for God to send the money, and start asking Him to open your eyes so that you can see what He's already sent. You'll find you'll get a lot farther a lot faster that way. The problem is not lack and poverty. The problem is your blindness, so ask God to open your eyes, and then roll up your sleeves and get to work.

That's one of the problems that I have with welfare. It's based on lack, on poverty. It's based on seeing myself as poor, broke, busted, and disgusted. How can I ever walk as a giant in my community when my eyes are blinded like that? How can I maximize the wealth and resources that come my way when I'm looking around and seeing nothing but need? Welfare helps create the blindness. It's a trap that takes away your power and keeps you in need.

If I can go to the government and it says it will match a million dollars to every million I receive from the private sector, then it's a good deal. But if it's just going to give me some money to do a program, then it's not going to work. That's what happened to welfare. We got comfortable on welfare, government money, government cheese and peanut butter and jelly. This poverty mentality created a generation of people who can't even get back into the workforce now that the government giving system no longer exists.

THE POWER OF RESOURCES THROUGH NETWORKING

Success is all about teamwork. It's all about working together as a team: husband, wife, friends, family, black, white, orange, purple—it doesn't make any difference. We're all in this together.

I'm proud of who I am, and I'm proud of the people I know. I have friends who sing, and I love to hear them. I'll put in a tape on my way to work and listen to one of my friends praise and worship God. She has a gift that she uses to build up others. Her gift builds me up, and that makes her a part of my team. When I get depressed, I need someone who can help me get into God's presence. This friend's music will do that for me.

It's her gift; it's why she was placed on this earth. What she gives to others through that gift is the way she is doing her part. She knows why she is walking on this earth. She's a part of the team.

Your gift makes you part of the same team. You were placed on this earth to have an effect larger than yourself. Your gifts are resources that can benefit the team.

There's an old African proverb that says, "It takes a village to raise a child." Well, we have to be careful today, because we never know who is in the village. There are strange, sinful people in the village now. Therefore, it takes more than a village. It takes a community of people who are committed to God and committed to one another to raise a child and provide a place where that child can maximize his or her potential. It takes all of us working together to get to where we need to go. We cannot get there alone, but we can get there together.

In our communities, we as individuals may not be able to get rid of drug dealers and malt liquor signs, but as a team, as a community, we can open or close the door at will. As a team, we have the power to say *no more*.

Jesus Christ took twelve people and changed the world. The doors are opening right now for faith-based people to join hands and make a difference in their communities, in this nation, and in the world.

Recently, I went to Washington, D.C., and witnessed the coming together of Baptists, Pentecostals, Catholics, and others in an effort to have an impact together that none could have alone.

God is speaking to you. You've held a vision in your heart for years, and now is the time to move forward. You can become a door to change in your community—perhaps not alone, but with others who are like-minded, you can reap the harvest of this generation before it rots on the ground. The harvest is ripe, and the choice is yours.

CHAPTER 10

MAXIMIZING THE MISSION, MANDATE, AND METHOD OF PURPOSE

When I worked at Denny's, I was an extremely successful franchisee. I was pumped up! One night, I left a leadership conference in the Bahamas with my friend and mentor, Dr. Myles Munroe, and stood looking out over a balcony of the Marriott Cable Beach Hotel, feeling just wonderful.

I was thinking, *I'm going to go back and buy the entire Michigan market. Man, I can do this. I'm going to get sixteen more restaurants.* I was looking out over the water, dreaming about expanding my vision even further and having more to give.

Suddenly, I heard the voice of God clearly in my spirit. He said, "You've done a great job. Well done, good and faithful servant. Now, I want you to go back and leave Denny's. I want you to sell your stores. I have something new in store for you."

It was the same voice that had spoken to me on my basement steps after I had been fired. I recognized it without discernment.

My first thought was to take my computer, turn on a nice CD, and drown out that voice. I started rebuking the devil: "Satan, you're a liar. In the name of Jesus, you get out of my hotel room."

A conflict began to take place inside my spirit that night, and it went on for six months. I couldn't sleep at night anymore. That voice would awaken me and tell me to sell the franchises. I was struggling to let go and obey God.

My stomach was constantly filled with butterflies—that feeling of apprehension. I just dreaded the thought of starting over again. I was ready to sit back and enjoy my success. I didn't want to go through the hard work of starting from ground zero once more.

I would pray, *Lord, I'm paying tithe. I'm sowing money. I'm a millionaire, Lord. The restaurant is producing very well, and they're getting ready to give me the entire Michigan market.*

Plagued by indecision, I did what most other men would have done. I asked my wife about it. But look how I positioned myself. I said, "Honey, the devil has been keeping me up all night long. He's been trying to get me to sell the restaurants. I need you to pray for me, and we need to come into covenant agreement together. He is trying to tell me to sell my Denny's, the gift that God gave me to show my enemies my footstool when I was being persecuted."

I made sure that Alena understood exactly where I stood in the entire matter.

Guess what? She said, "Honey, I've been feeling the same thing. Honey, whatever God is telling you to do, I'm here. I'm with you in it, just as I was before."

So I sold the restaurants I owned and embarked upon a new season and a new era in my life. God had done a great deal for me, and I knew that He had not brought me this far in order to hang me out to dry. He would be with me in this next level he was taking me to.

I called the Denny's corporation and told them what I was planning to do. Not unexpectedly, persecution, tests, and trials showed up. When you're getting ready to move into a new season or make quality decisions for the kingdom of God, it's common for such things to appear. Persecution and pressure always accompany decision-making time, and it hinders a lot of folks who are trying to advance to the next level.

You'll never advance to the next level without resistance and testing. It happens to us all, and it happened to me. Yeshua was led into the wilderness and was tempted and tested for authenticity three times by the devil. Once he passed those tests, His ministry began. There will be a new beginning for you if you can endure the test.

The company said, "Jerome, you can't leave. You're an icon, the first African-American franchisee, a role model. You're the person we fly all over the country. We'll give you another market if you stay, Jerome. We'll work out whatever you want if you will just stay and not leave."

Whoa, yet another market! They were preparing a table before me. Nevertheless, I knew that obedience to the voice and will of God was better than any carrot they could dangle before me. So I was obedient, and I walked away from that very tempting prize.

WHATEVER GOD CALLS FOR, HE PROVIDES RESOURCES FOR

If that wasn't enough of a test, God then told me to sow the largest check that I have ever sown into Dr. Myles

Munroe's ministry. It was the check from the largest business deal that I had ever received.

God told me to go to a conference and sow the largest portion of that check into the ministry of a man who had recently received some instructions from God about what he was to do. At that time in my walk with God, I didn't really understand a lot about sowing seed into what God was calling me into.

Nevertheless, I came to the leadership conference with the check. I kept it in my pocket until the final day of the conference. I was hoping that sometime during the week God would speak to me and release me from this command. However, He did not, and I sowed an enormous check into this other man's ministry.

As always, my wife was calm, cool, collected, and content. She knew what I had done, but she was completely unflappable.

I'll never forget the plane ride back home. For the entire trip I thought about what a fool I'd been, and how crazy it was to give away that much money. I never even saw the people on the plane beside me. All I could see was the new car I wouldn't be purchasing and the new house I wouldn't own.

Then, during that plane flight, God spoke again. "I want you to go buy this building and start Christian Business Network, and stop running it from your basement."

Does God have a sense of humor, or what? *I had the money to do that, but You told me to give it away. Remember, God?*

"What you had was not enough," He replied. "If you had used that, you would have accomplished it with your own power. I want to do this, and I want to show you something new."

I thought back to the time when all I had was $296.06 in my savings account to put toward a multi-million dollar Denny's franchise purchase. God had been faithful, and He had provided supernaturally for that endeavor.

So I entered into a new understanding of what it meant to be a seed sower. Every time an opportunity presented itself for me to give into someone's ministry, I obeyed God's promptings and gave. And every seed I planted has yielded a mighty harvest. The harvest that has come back to me is pressed down, shaken together, and running over.

YOU'RE ONLY GOING TO GET ONE CHANCE AT LIFE, SO LEAVE A LEGACY

Owning and running the restaurants had been God's MBA program. I had passed, and now I was ready to go forward towards my destiny. I was ready to impart the gifts of ownership, entrepreneurship, leadership, and management. I was ready to release a generation of other leaders, to multiply what God had done in me.

I had started Christian Business Network, which is a entrepreneurial training institute designed to build and release men and women into their communities as business owners and community leaders. Now God told me it was time me to perfect CBN.

Although the institute had only been in operation for a little over a year, we had already graduated more than forty entrepreneurs. Classes in our new Atlanta market are booked full for another two years.

My students have lavished awards and praises upon me. They have thanked me for making a dramatic difference in their lives, igniting passion within them, imparting the knowledge they need to succeed, and providing a vital network to connect them with other resources that can help them get started.

I've continued working as the owner of several businesses and financial endeavors. These entities help to support and finance Christian Business Network. CBN is my purpose. It's my *raison d'être*—reason for being—as the French would say. Christian Business Network is my legacy. Long after I'm gone there will be businesses flourishing in communities across this country that were birthed with the help of CBN.

The Bible says that God takes pleasure when we produce fruit in our lives, and that fruit remains. My legacy is what will live on after I die; it's what my life will be remembered for.

What is your legacy? What will live on after you, and what will continue to impact the world for the better long after you're gone? That's your legacy. If you haven't started to build your legacy, you need to start thinking about what it will be. You have a legacy; you have fruit from the purpose and giftedness of your life that will remain. It's up to you to learn what that is and to start building it.

BECOMING GOD'S PREVAILING PLAN

Today, I can recognize an environment in which to sow. Every seed I sow into a ministry or an individual's destiny, I extend with an assignment. One of my personal goals is to live debt-free, and I'm already seventy-five percent there. By the end of this year I plan to be completely debt-free. Recently, my mortgage company called me and said, "Do you know that you sent in a payment for $10,000?"

I said, "Yes, and you're going to get more. I'm paying it off."

"Well, Mr. Edmonson, the interest rates are down at three percent. There is really no need to pay it off now."

Once again, with any decision that will take you to the next level comes persecution, tests, and trials. I had made a decision to do this thing. God told me to do it, and look what happened. The mortgage bank wanted to send out a person to talk me out of it.

I told them that I didn't need to speak with any of their representatives, and they could simply send a letter with my payoff balance so that I could post it on my refrigerator and watch it decrease every month.

I'm focused, and when you're focused, nothing can stop you. When you're driven, you will get to where you want to go. But when you're not focused, you'll be pulled here and there by every wind that comes by.

When I was purchasing my building I had to renovate it. Therefore, I prayed for the funds. I was praying, "Lord, Father of Abraham, Isaac and Jacob, You gave me this building. I know you're going to give me the money to renovate it. Just show me the resources."

Do you know what? Those resources came. I was simply talking about my prayer to one of CBN's corporate sponsors, Mrs. Ray Hood-Phillips, chief diversity officer at Denny's, who is also a believer. After the conversation, she said that she had just received an unexpected bonus check and would bring it to the office. I received the check I had prayed for to cover all of my expenses for that building. God supplied the need supernaturally, from a source that I hadn't even considered. God works through people, but if you're afraid to talk about where you are, those sources cannot position themselves to help you.

For whatever God has called you to do, He will provide and supply all that you need to fulfill that call. Know this as well: that if He has called you, He took care of the need before you were born. Everything you need to succeed and achieve your destiny and purpose is waiting for you. The supply is there, ready and waiting for you to step forward and launch your plan.

MAXIMIZING YOUR POTENTIAL

Your success will be assured as you begin to discover your potential in God. That's where it all began for me. I read a book by Dr. Myles Munroe entitled *Understanding Your Potential*. After I read that book, I decided that I needed to contact him.

I realized that I had not even scratched the surface of the potential I had in God. Everything that I was still to become was inside of me, just waiting for an opportunity to express itself. I had been so busy focusing on what I had already accomplished that I wasn't even considering the untapped potential inside me. The same applies to you. You have vast resources, mighty gifts, and great abilities that are waiting for you to use them, to give them expression in the earth.

After I read Dr. Munroe's book, I realized that I needed to maximize the potential in my life and destiny. What I had experienced up to that point was but a small mustard seed, a grain of success, compared to the potential for success that was still inside of me waiting for an opportunity to grow.

I had nowhere to release the potential hidden inside of me. I had the potential to become a very influential individual. I had the potential to leave a legacy on Earth. I had enormous potential within me, and all I needed to do was to gain focus and allow that potential to find a place of expression.

That's when I realized the key to my life and my success was in maximizing—maximizing all of the resources God had given to me, internally and externally. I needed to seize the opportunities I had in the precious moments of living on this earth and use them to make a difference.

Do you realize that graveyards are full of unfulfilled potential, that thousands and millions of people walk the earth with resources inside of them that they never even realize are there? When they do realize they have potential, they never step out and give that potential a place of expression, a place to maximize itself.

I became determined that I would not be one more person who went to his grave filled with unfulfilled potential. I was determined to maximize my life, and that's what I've done.

Even in the ignorance of my youth, God was at work helping me to fulfill my potential. He was there for me with grace and mercy. He was on my side. All I had to do was dig down on the inside and discover what was there, the vast potential I had as a man created in God's image. I had to begin speaking to those things inside of me, calling them out, daring to dream and daring to boldly step out and believe that I could be more than I ever dreamed I could be, more than people said I would become.

You are no different. You were created for a purpose, with vast potential to do great things. All that you need to fulfill that potential is in you. It was ready for you at your birth. You already have, right now, the ability to do everything that God has called you to do.

Perhaps you have a mind-set that says, "I can't do this." Or, "Woe is me because I've had it tough." Or,

"God, why me? I hate this world." Or, "I'd rather be dead." These kinds of thoughts and beliefs will never help you maximize your potential.

You must call yourself what you are in God. You must believe in who He made you to be. You must cast off the negative, self-defeating words that you speak over yourself or that others have spoken over you all your life.

Remember, as a man thinketh in his heart, so is he (see Prov. 23:7). The law of association says you will become the top five people you associate with the most. Who controls your thinking? Determine within yourself right now that you will fill up your mind with God's thoughts about you. You will focus on your dream and your purpose, and you will put behind you the defeating self-talk that has dragged down your spirit and sabotaged your destiny for so long.

SHIFTING PARADIGMS AND CHANGING POWER SOURCES

As I've already mentioned, I believe that we are in a time of change. Paradigms and power sources are on the threshold of change. I'm convinced that we will see an enormous paradigm shift in African-American communities across the nation. The time for change is imminent.

Recently, at our Christian Business Network Black History Conference dinner, we discussed the issue of freedom within the African-American community and in the nation at large. We determined that in order to define freedom, we must first be prepared to locate and define its source. What I mean is this: if you let someone else become your source of freedom, then you have just lost it. When your source of freedom becomes one particular group of individuals, then you have turned your freedom over to that group. Those individuals now control your existence and destiny.

This has been the single greatest misconception and weakness of the African-American community. We continue to struggle with the civil rights movement and its issues, and we struggle with the power brokers who have been set in place by that era and movement. As the apostle Paul said of his people the Jews, my wife and I have great sorrow and anguish in our hearts continually because of the cultural and spiritual oppression that is imposed by these powers.

Our heart's desire and prayer for all African-American people is that they be delivered from the demonic belief that the government and other human sources or agencies hold the keys to their deliverance. As the sons and daughters of enslaved and oppressed people, we have had the literal chains on our hands and feet broken. But those chains were transferred to our minds and spirits by psychological intimidation and racist cultural propaganda. Now, many have passed on those psychological chains to a new generation of slaves.

Whatever you think about yourself, you will eventually become. If you see yourself as a business owner long enough, then that's what you will become. But if you think that you'll never have anything and you'll never own anything, then you never will. I always wanted to own my own business, and I thought about it often as a boy. As I thought, so I became.

I always wanted to be the best, so it didn't amaze me that when I was working for the world's largest chicken restaurant chain I led the nation in sales and profits. I was young and energetic, so the company moved all the white area managers out to the suburban restaurants and gave me the inner city. And I walked through those filthy, roach-infested restaurants as a change agent. I walked out my destiny as a businessman and entrepreneur.

FIRED UP—MAXIMIZE YOUR OWN MISFORTUNE

There's no doubt that you've probably been through many difficult, degrading, and debilitating events and situations in your life. We have all had our times of testing. Nevertheless, you have a great destiny. You've been called to accomplish great things, to leave a legacy and to be a change agent in your neighborhood, your family, your nation, and your world.

My wife and I have begun studying our Hebrew roots, and God has sent us a Jewish rabbi who has accepted Jesus Christ as Savior to teach us the original texts and language of the greatest CEO who ever lived, Yeshua Ha Maschia, Jesus the Christ.

We are moving toward our next level of success by developing a relationship with a resource of people, three percent of whose population controls eighty-five percent of our nation's wealth. I'm speaking about the Jewish community.

I believe that the reason you are holding this book in your hands is because you, too, are a man or woman of destiny. Your destiny is before you, and the choice is yours. Now is the time to seize your opportunity to shine so brightly, like a star in the sky, that this world begins to see your good works and glorify our Father in Heaven. Someone is depending on you to become all that God has called you to be. So step out, get fired up, and maximize the misfortune in your life.

I'LL SEE YOU AT THE TOP!

ABOUT THE AUTHOR

Jerome Edmondson is the Senior Partner of Edmondson Associates, Inc. an entrepreneur training and small business consulting firm. In 1995, Edmondson through his food service company A&W Food, Inc. was recognized as the nations first minority Denny's franchise owner graduate, and in 1998 he became the first black A&W franchise owner.

In August of 1998 Edmondson founded a non-profit business training and entrepreneur development organization called the Christian Business Network, Inc. (CBN), which is dedicated to raising the awareness of faith-based principles, standards of morality, integrity, character and ethics in business and the workplace. CBN host annual business summits and seminars with its vast circle of influence in the corporate and small business sector with a focus on bridging the gap for the next generation of youth leadership. Edmondson and CBN's business leaders meet month at their nationally expanding Business Training Centers and NxLevel Entrepreneur Training Institutes currently in Detroit and Atlanta.

Edmondson is admired by many because of his consistence display of love for his wife Alena and their children Cherita, Aaron and William.

Christian Business Network International
20825 Evergreen Road, Southfield, MI 48075
Phone # (248)357-9485 or Toll Free 877-CBN-4590
Fax: (248)357-9488
E-Mail: jerome@cbninternational.com

Additional copies of this book and other
book titles from DESTINY IMAGE are
available at your local bookstore.

For a complete list of our titles,
visit us at www.destinyimage.com
Send a request for a catalog to:

Destiny Image® Publishers, Inc.
P.O. Box 310
Shippensburg, PA 17257-0310

*"Speaking to the Purposes of God for This
Generation and for the Generations to Come"*